The Story of

Francis Loring Payne

Alpha Editions

This edition published in 2024

ISBN : 9789362995414

Design and Setting By
Alpha Editions
www.alphaedis.com
Email - info@alphaedis.com

As per information held with us this book is in Public Domain.
This book is a reproduction of an important historical work. Alpha Editions uses the best technology to reproduce historical work in the same manner it was first published to preserve its original nature. Any marks or number seen are left intentionally to preserve its true form.

Contents

FOREWORD THE HALL OF MIRRORS ....- 1 -

INTRODUCTION ....- 3 -

CHAPTER I THE BEGINNINGS OF VERSAILLES ....- 5 -

CHAPTER II THE MAKING OF VERSAILLES ....- 8 -

CHAPTER III THE LUXURY OF VERSAILLES ....- 14 -

CHAPTER IV THE GARDENS, THE FOUNTAINS AND THE GRAND TRIANON ....- 21 -

THE GRAND TRIANON ....- 28 -

CHAPTER V A DAY WITH THE SUN KING ....- 30 -

CHAPTER VI GOLDEN DAYS AND RED LETTER NIGHTS ....- 38 -

CHAPTER VII THE WOMEN OF VERSAILLES ....- 47 -

CHAPTER VIII THE VERSAILLES OF LOUIS XV ....- 55 -

CHAPTER IX THE TWILIGHT OF THE
BOURBON KINGS ....- 60 -

CHAPTER X THE SHRINE OF ROYAL
MEMORIES, THE SCENE OF WORLD
ADJUSTMENTS ....- 72 -

FOREWORD
THE HALL OF MIRRORS

I

If you could speak what tales your tongues could tell,
   You voiceless mirrors of the storied past!
Do you remember when the curtain fell
   On him who learned he was not God at last?

II

Do you still see the shadows of the great?
   On powdered wigs and velvets, silks and lace;
Or dream at night a feted queen, in state,
   Accepts men's homage with a haughty face?

III

A thousand names come tumbling to the mind.
   Of dead who gazed upon themselves through you.
And went their way, each one his end to find
   In paths that glory or red terror knew.

IV

Voltaire and Rousseau and Ben Franklin here,
   You've seen hobnobbing with the highly-born;
Seen Genius smile, while, with a hint of fear,
   It gave to Birth not homage but its scorn.

V

Do you remember that Teutonic jaw
   Of him who crowned an emperor, that you
Might know that Bismarck was above all law
   And free to do what victor vandals do?

VI

Oh, Hall of Visions, now shall come anon
   A grander sight than you have ever seen;
You've mirrored kings, but you shall look upon
   The mighty men whose edicts freedom mean

VII

To races and to peoples sore oppressed;
   The men who mould the future for a race
That breathes a wind that's blowing from the West--
   And you'll forget the Bourbon's evil face!

     --EDWARD S. VAN ZILE.
     N. Y. Eve. Sun., Nov. 25

INTRODUCTION

A TRAVELER'S REFLECTIONS ON VERSAILLES

From the low heights of Satory we get a complete view of the plains of Versailles--the woods, the town and the sumptuous chateau. The palace on its dais rules the scene. The village and ornamental environment have been constructed to augment its majesty. Even the soil has been "molded into new forms" at a monarch's caprice. Versailles is the expression of monarchy, as conceived by Louis XIV. It is the only epic produced in his reign--a reign so fertile in the other forms of poetry, and in talent of all kinds. What epic ever chronicled the destiny of an epoch in a manner more brilliant and complete? In this poem of stone the manners of heroic and familiar life mingle at every step. Besides the halls and galleries, the theaters of royal estate, there are mysterious passages and sequestered nooks that whisper a thousand secret histories. The palace has two voices, one grave and one gay and trifling. It is full of truths and fictions, tears and smiles. The personages of its drama are as various as life itself; kings, poets, ministers, courtiers, confessors, courtesans, queens without power, and queens with too much power; ambassadors, generals, little abbés and great ladies; nobles, clergy, even the people. For two centuries did this crowd continue to pass and re-pass over these marble floors and under these gilded vaults; and every day its flood became more impetuous, every day it gave way more and more to the whims and passions. And the palace heard all, saw all, spied all--and has retained all, each action in its acted hour, each word in its place. During the two centuries of absolute monarchy, nothing took place that Versailles did not either originate or answer. Every shot that was fired in Flanders, Germany and Spain awakened here an echo. Richelieu was here, the first statesman of the monarchy, and Necker, the last. French literary history is inscribed on its walls, which received within them the great writers of France from Molière to Beaumarchais. Art erected especially for Versailles the schools and systems whose influence has been felt through the succeeding centuries. For Versailles, Lebrun became a painter, Coysevox a sculptor, and Mansard an architect. But it was not France alone that depended on Versailles. Foreign nations sent their representatives to this famous center; the choice spirits of Europe came to visit it.

The history of Versailles was for two centuries the history of civilization. From Versailles may be seen the movement of manners, wars, diplomacy, literature, arts and energies that agitated Europe.

On entering Versailles by the Paris avenue, we see the palace on the summit of the horizon. The houses, scattered here and there and concealed among the trees, appear less to form a town than to accompany the monument raised beyond and above them. Approaching the Place d'Armes, we distinguish the different parts of which the imposing mass of buildings is composed. In the center is a singular bit of architecture. In vain the neighboring masses extend their circle around it: their great arms are unable to stifle it; but it possesses a seriousness of character that attracts the eye more strongly than their high white walls. This is the remains of the château built by Louis XIII at Versailles. Louis XIV did not wish to bury his father's dwelling.

CHAPTER I
THE BEGINNINGS OF VERSAILLES

A dreary expanse of low-lying marsh-land, dismal, gloomy and full of quicksands, where the only objects that relieved the eye were the crumbling walls of old farm buildings, and a lonely windmill, standing on a roll of higher ground and stretching its gaunt arms toward the sky as if in mute appeal against its desolate surroundings--such was Versailles in 1624. This uninviting spot was situated eleven miles southwest of Paris, the capital city of France, the royal city, the seat, during a century before, of the splendid court of the brilliant Francis I and of the stout-hearted Henry II, the scene of the masterful rule of Catherine de Medici, of the career of the engaging and beautiful Marguerite de Valois and of the exploits of the gallant Henry of Navarre.

The desolate stretch of marshland, with its lonely windmill, meant nothing then to the court nor to the busy fortune-hunting and pleasure-seeking inhabitants of Paris. No one had reason to go to Versailles, except perhaps the poor farmers and the owner of the isolated mill--least of all the nobility and fashionable folk of the glittering capital. No exercise of the imagination could then have conjured up the picture of the splendor in store for the barren waste of Versailles. The mention of the name in 1600 would have brought nothing more from the lips of royalty and nobility than an indifferent inquiry: "And what, pray, is Versailles and where may it be?" You, my lord, who raise your eyebrows interrogatingly, and you, my lady, who flick your fan so carelessly, will some day behold your grandchildren paying humble and obsequious court to the reigning favorites at Versailles--yes, out there on this very moorland where you see nothing but marshy hollows and ruined walls, there will your lord and master, your glorious Sun King, the Grand Monarch, Louis the Fourteenth, build a palace home that Belshazzar might justly have envied: there will he hold high court and set the whole world agape at his prodigal outlay and magnificent festivities. And well may we inquire to-day: how came this dreary waste to be the wondrous Versailles, the seat and scene of so much in the making and the making-over of the world?

Ancient records of France indicate that in 1065 the priory of St. Julien was established on the estates of the house of Versaliis--a grant under royal protection. A poor farm community grew up about the ecclesiastical retreat. Here, also, on the estates of the barony of Versailles, was a repair of lepers, destroyed in the sixteenth century.

The origin of the name is said by some to be derived from the fact that the plains thereabouts were exposed to such high winds that the grain in the poor land was frequently overturned (_versés_). The lord of these acres first named in history is Hugues (Hugo) de Versaliïs, who lived early in the eleventh century and was a contemporary of the first kings of the Capet dynasty. A long line of nobles of this family succeeded him. In 1561 Martial de Léomenie, Secretary of Finance under Charles IX, became master of Versailles. The farming village being on the route between Paris and Brittany, he obtained from the king permission to establish here four annual fairs and a weekly market on Thursdays. Martial perished in the Massacre of St. Bartholomew in 1572. Henry IV, as a prince, when hunting the stag with Martial often swept across the low plains of Versailles. The rights to the lands of the barony were acquired by Maréchal de Retz from the children of Martial de Léomenie, and inherited from the noble duke by his son, Jean-François de Gondi, first archbishop of France. It was this prelate that sold to Louis XIII in 1632, for 66,000 pounds (about $27,400), the land and barony of Versailles, consisting, in the phrase of the original deed, "of an old house in ruins and a farm with several buildings."

In 1624, Louis XIII, who had hunted in the vicinity of Versailles since childhood and in later life had sought relief there from ennui and melancholy, often slept in a low inn or in the hill-top windmill after long hunts in the forest of St. Leger. It occurred to him that it would be convenient for him to have a pavilion or hunting-lodge in this unattractive place, and accordingly he ordered one erected at Versailles, on the road that led to the forest of St. Leger. In 1627, concluding that in no other domain of its limited acreage could he find so great variety of land over which to hunt on foot and horse-back, he bought a small piece of property at Versailles. Immediately afterwards he caused to be erected what Saint-Simon called "a little house of cards" on the isolated hill that rolled up in the heart of the valley, where the windmill had stood.

Louis' architect was Philbert Le Roy, and the new villa was about two hundred feet from the lodge first constructed. Its form was a complete square, each corner being terminated by a tower. The building was of brick, ornamented with columns and gilded balustrades; it was surrounded by a park adorned with statues sculptured after designs by the artist Poussin. Ambitious addition! A villa on the old mill site, decorated by the favorite court artist of the day, Nicolas Poussin! The court resented the enterprise, the nobility despised it. It was the King's fancy; nothing else excused it. A noble of the court, Bassompierre, exclaimed that "it was a wretched château in the construction of which no private gentleman could be vain."

Scarcely was his new chateau finished (1630) when the King took up his residence there for the hunt. In this place were terminated in November,

1630, the autocratic services of Cardinal Richelieu to the King--the first of many significant historical events to take place there.

The King's sojourns at Versailles during the hunting season, however, had their effect. Many of the royal intimates were influenced to build on land given to them by the sovereign. So before Louis XIII died his chateau was surrounded by many charming country houses. On April 8, 1632, Louis came into possession of the feudal dwelling of Jean-François de Gondi and its lands. Versailles then began to acquire distinction. It was the King's resort. Could any one afford to question its character, or location, or the standing of those that, at the King's behest, took up their residence there? Not we surely, who can now view Versailles in the light of history. All aside from its splendid court life and its magnificent festivities, we know it as the scene of three epoch-making events in the world's history. During and shortly after the American Revolution, Versailles was the scene of treaty negotiations in which France, England and America were the active parties. About a century later, in 1871, the treaty was consummated there that ended the Franco-Prussian War, by which France lost Alsace and Lorraine and was forced to pay to Germany $1,000,000,000. And now, in our day, the most superb irony of history has brought about a treaty in the same Hall of Mirrors by which Germany repays, and the map of Europe undergoes radical changes.

CHAPTER II
THE MAKING OF VERSAILLES

The Luxurious Château and Parkland of Louis XIV

At the death of Louis XIII, in 1643, the little château of Versailles was abandoned as a dwelling. Then followed a fall in values at Versailles and a great flutter of uncertainty among those that had followed the King there. This feeling of doubt lasted for seven years. The faces of the court favorites were turned back toward Paris, and individual fortunes were speculatively weighed in the balance with the possibilities of the new King's whims and fancies. But when the twelve-year-old Louis XIV came to hunt in the vicinity of Versailles for the first time, he found the suburban dwelling of his father attractive from the start. The Gazette noted this visit, in 1651, and described the supper that the royal boy shared with the officials of the chateau. Two months later the King supped again at Versailles, and was so delighted with the estate and the hunting to be had thereabouts that, thereafter, he made it a yearly custom to visit Versailles once or twice in the hunting season, sometimes with his brother, sometimes with his prime minister, Cardinal Mazarin.

Returning in 1652 from an interview at Corbeil with Charles II of England, then seeking refuge in France, Louis XIV dined at Versailles with his mother, Anne of Austria. In October, 1660, four months after his marriage to Maria Theresa of Spain, he brought his young queen there. The future of Versailles was assured. The King had decided to set his star and make his palace home where his father had established a hunting lodge.

The year 1661 was one of the most important in the history of the monarch. On March fifteenth, eight days after the death of Mazarin, the great Colbert was named Superintendent of Finances. It was he who was to give to the reign of Louis XIV its definite direction; his name was to be lastingly associated with the founding of the greater Versailles, and with the construction of the Louvre, the Tuileries, Fontainebleau and Saint-Germain. But Colbert's task in the enlargement of Versailles was no easy one, nor did he approve of it. He opposed the young King's purpose obstinately and expressed himself on the subject without reserve. "Your majesty knows," he wrote to the King, "that, apart from brilliant actions in war, nothing marks better the grandeur and genius of princes than their buildings, and that posterity measures them by the standard of the superb edifices that they erect during their lives. Oh, what a pity that the greatest king, and the most virtuous, should be measured by the standard of Versailles! And there is always this misfortune to fear."

But the King, like many another great monarch, had dreamed a dream. He was not satisfied with Paris as a residence. So he told Colbert to make his dream of Versailles come true--and Colbert had to find some way to pay the cost.

An irritating cause of the King's purpose lay in the fact that he was incited by the splendors of the chateau of Vaux-le-Vicomte, built by his ill-fated minister, Fouquet. Louis determined to surpass that mansion by one so much more elaborate as to crush it into insignificance. Nicholas Fouquet had employed the most renowned masters of this period--among them Louis Le Vau, the architect, André Le Nôtre, the landscape gardener, and Charles Lebrun, the decorator. These were the men the King summoned to transform the modest hunting villa of his father. At the truly gorgeous chateau of his minister, he had witnessed the full measure of their genius. On August 17, 1661, Fouquet gave an elaborate fête to celebrate the completion of the chateau, which the King attended. Within three weeks the host was a prisoner of State, accused of peculation in office. Acting immediately upon his resolution to out-do the glories of Vaux-le-Vicomte, Louis engaged Le Nôtre to plan gardens and Le Vau to submit proposals for the enlargement and decoration of the chateau. One of the first apartments completed was the chamber of the infant Dauphin--heir to the throne, who was born in November, 1661. Colbert reported in September, 1663, that in two years he had spent 1,500,000 pounds, and a good part of this sum was for the construction of the gardens. Builders and decorators suggested one elaborate project after another, without regard to the cost, despite the protest of Colbert to the King that they were exceeding all estimates and provisions. It was a paradise period for profiteers.

Versailles became a favorite retreat of the extravagant young sovereign. He frequently drove out from Paris, and on sundry occasions gave splendid balls and dinners.

For periods of increasing frequency the King was in residence at Versailles. He urged on the builders who had in hand the construction of the living-rooms, kitchens, stables; he supervised the placing of pictures and other decorative works in various parts of the expanded chateau; impatiently he chided the superintendents for delay and feverishly they strove to meet his demands for greater haste. And though every hour of haste cost the King of France a substantial sum, he cared for nothing but the fulfillment of his luxurious plans. Hundreds of laborers were engaged in laying out the orangery, the grand terrace, the fruit and vegetable gardens. The original entrance court was greatly enlarged. Long wings terminated by pavilions bordered it. On the right were the kitchens, with quarters for the domestics; on the left, the stables, where there were stalls for fifty-four horses. At the main entrance to the court were pavilions used by the musketeers as guard-houses. Those were bustling times at Versailles, and every day disclosed a new development and opened the way to new miracles of construction.

And the miracles were wrought, one after another--all by order of the King. On the site of the park a great terrace was bordered by a parterre in the shape of a half-moon, where a waterfall was later installed. A long promenade, now called the Allée Royale, extended to a vast basin named the Lake of Apollo. Streamlets were diverted to feed fountains. Twelve hundred and fifty orange trees were transported from the fallen estate of Vaux to fill the long arcades of the orangery.

In the midst of the activities of masons, carpenters, gardeners, the King was dominant, directing minute details--the laying of floors, the hanging of draperies, the installation of art works in the chapel. The restive master of the estate was impatient to enjoy his creation, and to invite his Court there to celebrate its completion with fêtes both brilliant and costly. Colbert wrote in a letter dated September, 1663, of the beauty of the chateau's adornments--its Chinese filigree of gold and silver.

"Never," he swore, "had China itself seen so many examples of this work together--nor had all Italy seen so many flowers." Colbert suffered, but the King found royal satisfaction. The splendid scene of the Sun King must be set--the people had to pay. It was Colbert's affair to finance it.

The King commanded a series of fêtes to be arranged. For eight days every diversion appropriate to the autumn season was enjoyed by the royal family and all the Court. Every day there were balls, ballets, comedies, concerts, promenades, hunts. Molière and his troupe were commanded to appear in a new piece called "_Impromptu de Versailles_."

Colbert regretted the absorption of his sovereign in Versailles, "to the neglect of the Louvre--assuredly the most superb palace in the world." Louis tolerantly gave ear and inspected the Louvre, but to the building of Versailles he devoted all his enthusiasm.

The appearance of the villa erected by Louis XIII had been vastly altered as to its roofs, chimneys, facades. In 1665 the court was ornamented by the placing of the pedestals and busts that still surround it. In addition to the main edifice, the King gave orders for the building of small dwellings to be occupied by favorites of his entourage, and by musicians, actors and cooks. Three broad tree-lined avenues were laid out and the highway to Paris--the Cours-la-Reine--commenced. Already Versailles took on a more imposing aspect than ancient Fontainebleau. Workmen were constantly busy with the building of reservoirs, the laying of sod, the planting of labyrinths, hedges, secret paths and bosky retreats, with the setting out of hundreds of trees brought from Normandy, and the seeding of flower gardens of surpassing beauty. Ponds, fountains, grottoes, waterfalls and straying brooks came into being at the command of the ambitious young ruler. At some distance from the chateau courts and cages were constructed to shelter rare birds and animals. It was designed that this should be "the most splendid palace of animals in the world." The King decided the details of building and decoration and supervised the installation of the furred and feathered tenants of the palatial menagerie. This was the enclosure so greatly admired by La Fontaine, Racine and Boileau, during a visit to Versailles in 1668.

The first epoch of the construction of Louis XIV coincided with the first sculptural decoration of Versailles. A great number of works of art were ordered for the adornment of the walks and gardens. Many statues and busts of mythological subjects that were made at Rome to the order of Fouquet, after models by Nicolas Poussin, were removed from Vaux to Versailles. That was a thriving period for sculptors of France and adjacent countries. Records faithfully kept by Colbert detail expenditures of thousands of pounds of the nation's money for bronze vases, stone figures of nymphs and dryads and dancing fauns that were placed among the trees and fountains of Versailles. Much of the ornamental sculpture ordered at this time disappeared from the royal domain, as Louis XIV constantly demanded the work of the newest artists and all the novelties of the moment.

By the year 1668 Versailles apparently approached completion. It had then been seven years in building. But in 1669 the general character of the chateau was again changed. In the embellishments proposed by Le Vau, the architect, the royal domain became the scene of renewed activity, engendered by the King, then just turned thirty years of age, and eager to achieve still greater improvements at Versailles to mark the increasing prosperity of his reign. Half-finished buildings were demolished and begun anew. Immense structures arose, and once again artists flocked to Versailles. Inside the palace and in the park they wrought an elaborate scheme of decoration that made this the most sumptuous dwelling of the monarchy. In the words of Madame Scudery, an annalist of that epoch, Versailles, under the new orders of the King, became "incomparably more beautiful." Another Versailles was born; at the same time there was created a town on the vast acres purchased by the King, in the midst of which three great avenues were built, converging toward the chateau. In addition to the enlargement and improvement of the palace, the King ordered the erection of houses for the use of Colbert, now superintendent of the royal buildings, and for the officers of the Chancellery. From this time he interested himself particularly in the advancement of the infant town; he bought the village of "Old Versailles" and made liberal grants of land to individuals who agreed to build houses there. Opposite the chateau arose the mansions of illustrious nobles of the Court.

As the King remained obstinate in his determination that the "little chateau" of his father should not be removed to make room for a structure more in harmony with the surrounding ostentation, Le Vau covered over the moats and built around the lodge of Louis XIII with imposing effect. The new buildings containing the state apartments of the King and Queen and public salons were separated by great courts from the insignificant beginning of all this mounting splendor. Le Vau did not live to see the completion of the palace. He died in 1670. The work of reconstruction, in which the King maintained a lively interest whether at home or abroad, was continued by the architect's pupils at a cost of thousands of pounds. Eagerly Louis read plans and listened to reports. With still greater interest he attended the proposals of the great Mansard--nephew of the designer and builder who in 1650 revived the use of the "Mansard roof." When he succeeded as "first architect," Jules Mansard (or Mansart) first undertook the erection of quarters for the Bourbon princes. In the same year (1679) that he began the immense south wing for their use, he gave instructions for the building of the now historic Hall of Mirrors between two pavilions named--most appropriately in the light of after events--the Salon of Peace and the Salon of War. From the high arched windows of this glittering Grand Gallery great personages of past and present epochs have surveyed the gardens, fountains and broad walks that are the crowning glory of Versailles.

In the time of the Grand Monarque more than a thousand jets of water cast their silver spray against the greenery of hedge and grove. "Nothing is more surprising," said a chronicler of Louis the Fourteenth's reign, "than the immense quantity of water thrown up by the fountains when they all play together at the promenades of the King. These jets are capable of using up a river." A writer of our day bids us pause for a moment at the viewpoint in the gardens most admired by the King--at the end of the Allée of Latona. "To the east, beyond the brilliant parterre of Latona, with its fountains, its flowers, and its orange-trees, rise the vine-covered walls of the terraces, with their spacious flights of steps and their vividly green clipped yews. Turn to the west and survey the Royal Allée, the Basin of Apollo, and the Grand Canal, or look to the north to the Allée of Ceres, or to the south to that of Bacchus, and you realize the harmony that existed between Mansard and Le Nôtre in the decoration of the chateau and in the plan of the gardens." Beyond the palace and the surrounding gardens lay the park in which the Grand Trianon was built, of marble, near the bank of the Grand Canal. Madame de Maintenon, who became the King's second wife, was housed within these sumptuous walls, which were completed in 1688.

And so the construction of this miracle work of the Great Monarch went on. In Versailles, Louis was bent on realizing himself, and nothing but himself. The Pharaoh of Egypt built his pyramids with as little consideration of what it meant in tribute from his subjects. Each year took its toll in money and men to make this home of Louis the Magnificent. "The King," wrote Madame de Sévigné on the twelfth of October, 1678, "wishes to go on Saturday to Versailles, but it seems that God does not wish it, by the impossibility of putting the buildings in a state to receive him, and by the great mortality among the workmen." But the work had continued, as the King commanded, and when he finally entered into possession of his new palace in 1682 with all his Court, thirty-six thousand men and six thousand horses were still engaged in making matters comfortable and satisfactory for His Glorious Majesty. "The State," exclaimed the Sun King, "it is I!" and in the same mood he might have added, "Versailles--it is the State!"

CHAPTER III
THE LUXURY OF VERSAILLES

The Splendors of the Château--its Apartments and Gardens, the Hall of Mirrors

In planning the interior decorations at Versailles, the numerous company of artists employed by the sovereign devised a scheme of ornamentation inspired by the arts of ancient Rome. Mythological and historical subjects were utilized for the glorification of the Grand Monarch. A _Description_ of the château, officially printed in 1674, gives us the key to the interpretation of the allegories. "As the Sun is the device of the King, and poets represent the Sun and Apollo as one, nothing exists in this superb dwelling that does not bear relation to the Sun divinity."

The emblem of Apollo was in evidence everywhere; signs of the month ornamented facades and walls; and inside the palace and out were symbols of the seasons and the hours of the day. The King's apartment bore on its ceiling and walls paintings depicting deeds of seven heroes of Antiquity, supported by Louis' planet emblem. All the interior decoration was Italian in style--marble wainscoting in window embrasures, floors of marble, panels of marble, doors of repoussé bronze. The apartments of Anne of Austria and the Gallery of Apollo at the Louvre offered the first examples in France of this decorative style, and guided the artists at Versailles in making their plans.

Upon the Grand Apartments of the King and Queen alone, a dozen painters were engaged between the years 1671 and 1680. Charles Lebrun directed the artists, most of whom, be it said, were poor colorists. He himself worked on the vault above the Stairway of the Ambassadors and in the Hall of Mirrors. To imitate Italian works of art was at that time the avowed ideal of French decorators. At Rome the King's purse paid the expenses of a group of young artists who were allotted the task of copying designs that were later evolved at Versailles. To some was assigned the copying of ornaments made of metal, mosaic and inlay. Others specialized on bronze and wood-carving designs. There were painters who made only sketches of battle scenes and sieges. There were sculptors on the King's staff of copyists, and goldsmiths, and enamel workers. Flemish, Dutch, French, but principally Italian, craftsmen were recruited from the art centers of Europe, "for the glory of the King." At the Gobelin Tapestry Factory--a royal establishment--the workers were directed by Charles Lebrun, who for many years had been head of the "Royal Manufactory of Crown Furniture."

It was in the year 1677 that Louis XIV formally proclaimed Versailles his residence and the seat of Government. It was for the purpose of providing quarters for the Court and its attendants that Mansard was commanded to enlarge the château. Versailles now became, in truth, the temple of royalty. The newly appointed architect gave to the chateau its final aspect; the stamp of his genius rests upon the exterior design and interior embellishment of the most remarkable dwelling in the history of French architecture.

[Illustration: Versailles]

When the Court came to live at Versailles in May, 1682, Mansard and his builders were still feverishly occupied in the work of construction and reconstruction. The year 1684 saw the end of the ornamentation of the interior in the completion of the Hall of Mirrors. Mansard's style is particularly impressed upon the Marble Stairway, and the adjacent Hall of the Queen's Guards, and, above all, on the Grand Gallery of the Mirrors and the Salons (Peace and War) that flank it--works truly impressive in their proportions, adornment and arrangement.

Disposed about three sides of the main court, the red château was set low on a slight rise of land. The main entrance was flanked by the North Wing and the South Wing, interrupted throughout their length by lesser courts. The domed chapel upreared to the right of the gate was the fourth one to serve the palace. After a period of building lasting ten years it was consecrated in the year 1710. The exquisite white stone edifice is still regarded as an architectural gem. Its interior embellishments were carried out by some of the best artists of the Sun King's epoch. Here during the last years of his long and spectacular reign, Louis the Great worshiped. Here Marie Antoinette was married to the Sixteenth Louis.

Arrivals at the palace were admitted from the Place d'Armes to the court designated for their reception. Only the King and his family might enter by the central gate. Nobles passed through the gates at the side. Privileged persons were permitted to alight in the Royal Court; those of inferior prestige in the Court of the Ministers, which gave entrance to the offices and living quarters of the palace executives and the hundreds of minions composing the King's retinue. On the left of the enclosure called the Marble Court was the vestibule to the Marble Stairway; opposite was the doorway leading to the renowned Stairway of the Ambassadors, later removed by command of Louis XV. The royal suites, except those of the Dauphin and his attendants, were on the second floor. These rooms beneath the ornate Mansard attic were the scene of all the potent events and ceremonies that have distinguished Versailles above the palaces of the world.

Grouped above the Marble Court at the far end of the main court of the château, were the State Apartments of the King. Though, in later times, the sequence of some of these salons was changed, in the years when the Sun King occupied them they comprised the Salon of Venus, opening upon the Ambassadors' Staircase, the Salon of Diana, the Salon of Mars, and the Salon of Mercury. These halls formed a magnificent prelude to the still greater magnificence of the Salon of Apollo,--the Throne Room where guests came into the presence of the King himself. The Salon of Venus was most admired for its marble mosaics and its ceiling painting representing Venus subduing all the other deities. In Louis' day, as now, the royal master of all this grandeur was here portrayed in white marble, garbed in the robes of a Roman emperor. Diana and her nymphs were depicted on the ceiling of the salon named for the Goddess of the Hunt. Here under candles glimmering in sconces of silver and crystal the courtiers engaged in games of billiards, while their ladies disposed themselves gracefully upon tapestried seats. And there were orange trees in silver tubs to add brilliance to the scene. In the Salon of Mars dancing parties and concerts were given. Silver punchbowls set on silver tables offered refreshment to the gay throng that coquetted and danced and applauded beneath the triumphant picture of Mars limned upon the ceiling. This room was a-glitter with silver, cut glass and gold embroidered draperies. In the crimson-hung Salon of Mercury was the King's bed of state, before which was a balustrade of silver. In all the Grand Apartments were hangings and furniture of extraordinary richness. There were tables of gilded wood and mosaic, Florentine marbles, pedestals of porphyry for vases of precious metal, ebony cabinets inlaid with copper, columns of jasper, agate and lapis lazuli, silver chandeliers, branched candle-sticks, baskets, vessels for liqueurs, silver perfuming pans. Windows were draped with silver brocade worked in gold thread, with Venetian silks and satins, or embroideries from the Gobelin studios. On the floors, originally of marble, were spread carpets woven in designs symbolical of kingly power.

The Throne Room known as the Salon of Apollo--the seat of the Sun King--was of the utmost richness. The throne itself was of silver and stood eight feet high. Tapestries represented scenes of splendor in the life of Louis the Great and on the walls were masterpieces by Italian artists of the first rank, which were later deemed worthy of a place in the Louvre. Much of the treasure vanished in the years 1689-1690 when the King was constrained to raise money for his depleted treasury. In December, 1682, the _Mercure Galant_, desirous of pleasing its readers, always avid of details about everything that concerned their King, published a long description of the furnishings of the State Apartments--the velvet hangings, the marble walls enriched with gold relief, the chimney-pieces bossed with silver.

Yet the glory of these apartments was outdone by the later achievements of architect and decorators in the Salons of War and Peace and the Hall of Mirrors that joins them. In the cupola of the Salon of War the great Lebrun painted an allegorical picture of France hurling thunderbolts and carrying a shield blazoned with the portrait of King Louis, while Bellona, Spain, Holland and Germany are shown crouching in awe. The colored marbles of the walls contrasted brilliantly with gilded copper bas-reliefs. Six portraits of Roman emperors contributed to the impressiveness of the Salon, and on the wall was a stucco relief of the King of France on horseback, clad like a Roman. The Salon of Peace was also decorated by Lebrun's adept brush. A ceiling piece portrays France and her conquered enemies rejoicing in the fruits of Peace. And, again, there are portraits of the ever-present Louis and the Caesars of Rome. Both these splendid halls remain to-day much as they were in the time of their creator.

Most lavish is the decoration of the Grand Hall of Mirrors--"the epitome of absolutism and divine right and the grandeur of the House of Bourbon." For two hundred and forty feet it extends along the terrace that surveys the gardens where Louis XIV and his successors delighted to ordain fêtes of unimaginable gayety. Gorgeously costumed courtiers, women that dictated the fate of dynasties, diplomats of our day bent upon the solution of world-rocking problems, all have gazed from this resplendent gallery upon the fountains and allées that beautify the scene below. Seventeen lofty windows are matched by as many Venetian framed mirrors. Between each window and each mirror are pilasters designed by Coyzevox, Tubi and Caffieri--reigning masters of their time. Walls are of marble embellished with bronze-gilt trophies; large niches contain statues in the antique style. The gilded cornice is by Coyzevox, the ceiling by Lebrun. The conception of the latter comprises more than a score of paintings representing events that had to do with wars waged by Louis the Great against Holland, Germany and Spain. In the period when Versailles was the residence of kings--not a museum, alone, and the assembly-place of international Councils--the tables in the Grand Gallery, the benches between the windows, the many-branched candelabra, the tubs in which orange trees grew, were all of heavy silver. Thousands of wax candles lighted the salon, some of them set in immense chandeliers, others in lusters of silver and crystal. But Louis the Fourteenth's reign was not yet over when he was compelled to send many hundred pieces of his precious furniture to the mint, and the superb appointments of the Hall of Mirrors were partially substituted by furnishings of wood and damask.

[Illustration: The Hall of Mirrors]

Visitors to Versailles view the private or "little" apartments of King Louis the Great, Louis XV and Louis XVI. The superb bedchamber of Louis XIV contains the bed in which the French Monarch died on September 1, 1715. In an ante-chamber, later called the Bull's Eye by reason of its unique oval window, courtiers were wont to gossip and intrigue while they awaited the King's rising. A quaint painting by a French artist presents Louis XIV and his family in the character of pagan deities. Next to the Bull's Eye was the room in which the King dined on occasion. The Hall of the King's Guards was near of approach to the Marble Staircase and to the ample and ornate apartments of Madame de Maintenon. The wonders of this Hall are also departed. In a group of small rooms were rich stores of objects of art, medals, cameos, onyx, bronzes, and gems of great value.

The State Apartments of the Queens of France were entirely altered in their decoration as one queen succeeded another. Marie Thérèse was the first to occupy them. We are told that before her bed there stood a railing of silver, that later gave way, for economical reasons, to one carved in wood. In the Grand Cabinet the wife of Louis the Great received in audience those that the King commanded. Here, at the end of a short and insignificant period as mistress of Versailles, Marie Thérèse died, July 30, 1683.

One of the few apartments that still retains the aspect it bore in King Louis the Fourteenth's reign is the Hall of the Queen's Guards, which had a door on the landing of the marble stair, also called the Queen's Staircase. This was the flight of steps most used in the time of Louis, since it led to the apartments of the sovereign, the Queen Madame de Maintenon.

The Ambassadors' Staircase, across the court, was of the richest possible decoration, but like the glory of the Kings of France, it has passed into oblivion. Louis commanded that it be paved and walled in marble from the choicest quarries, vaulted with bronze, graced by fountains. Amazing frescoes representing a brilliant assemblage of people of all nations adorned the walls. Of this staircase a reporter of the epoch wrote, "When full of light it vies in magnificence with the richest apartments of the most beautiful palace in the world." Which palace was, of course, Versailles.

The Grand Hall of the Guards, the apartments of the Children of France and their governess, the ten rooms that composed the suite of the Dauphin, the Grand Hall of Battles--each had its special decoration. "At the house of Monseigneur," wrote an old chronicler of the Court, "one sees in the cabinets an exquisite collection of all that is most rare and precious, not only in respect to the necessary furniture, tables, porcelains, mirrors, chandeliers, but also paintings by the most famous masters, bronzes, vases of agate, jewels and cameos." For one dazzling table of carved silver in the apartment of the King's son, the silversmith that fashioned it was paid thirty thousand dollars.

Beneath the state apartments of the King was the Hall of the Baths lined with marble and adorned with beautiful paintings. Upon the marble tubs, the tessellated floors, the gilded columns and mirrors of this apartment a great sum was expended.

* * * * *

Versailles at last was finished--and what a spectacle and monument to selfish exaltation it was! "There is an intimate relation between the King and his château," wrote Imbert de Saint-Amand. "The idol is worthy of the temple, the temple of the idol. There is always something immaterial, something moral so to speak, in monuments, and they derive their poesy from the thought connected with them. For a cathedral, it is the idea of God. For Versailles, it is the idea of the King. Its mythology is but a magnificent allegory of which Louis XIV is the reality. It is he always and everywhere. Fabulous heroes and divinities impart their attributes to him or mingle with his courtiers. In honor of him, Neptune sheds broadcast the waters that cross in air in sparkling arches. Apollo, his favorite symbol, presides over this enchanted world as the god of light, the inspirer of the muses; the sun of the god seems to pale before that of the great King.

Nature and art combine to celebrate the glory of the sovereign by a perpetual hosannah. All that generations of kings have amassed in pictures, statues and precious movables is distributed as mere furniture in the glittering apartments of the chateau. The intoxicating perfumes of luxury and power throw one into a sort of ecstasy that makes comprehensible the exaltation of this monarch, enthusiastic over himself, who, in chanting the hymns composed in his praise, shed tears of admiration."

CHAPTER IV
THE GARDENS, THE FOUNTAINS AND THE GRAND TRIANON

The first gardens of Versailles--those that gave a modest setting to the villa constructed for Louis XIII, comprised a few parterres of flowers and shrubs bounded by well trimmed box hedges, and two groves planted on each side of the _Allée Royale_. To Jacques Boyceau is accredited the first plan of the gardens of Versailles, but Andre Le Nôtre greatly amplified and improved the original scheme. Le Nôtre's achievements at Versailles gave him rank as the most distinguished landscape gardener of his time, and of all time.

Besides the luxurious and symmetrical gardens at Versailles, he originated the designs of those at the royal houses at Trianon, Saint-Cloud, Merly, Clagny, Chantilly and the Tuileries. The Parterre of the Tiber at Fontainebleau also added to his high reputation. For a long period the style of garden perfected by Le Nôtre was taken as a model and imitated throughout Europe. In 1678 he went to Italy on a mission for the King, who desired him to make researches there. While at Rome the eminent artist from France was commissioned to plan the gardens of the Quirinal, the Vatican and the villas Ludovisi and Albani. The Elector of Brandenburg summoned him to design the garden at Oranienburg; Kensington Park in London is still another example of Le Nôtre's skill. In his genius were reflected the qualities that distinguished the art of his century: regularity of design, harmony, dignity and richness of materials. Louis XIV had an enduring admiration for the work and character of the Chief Gardener--a man at all times honest, retiring, and inspired by enthusiasm for his calling.

We are told by a French chronicler that "when Le Nôtre had traced out his ideas, he brought Louis XIV to the spot to judge the distribution of the principal parts of their ornamentation. He began with two grand basins which are on the terrace in front of the chateau, with their magnificent decorations. He explained next his idea of the double flight of stairs, which is opposite the center of the palace, adorned with yew-trees and with statues, and gave in detail all the pieces that were to enrich the space that it included. He passed then to the _Allée du Tapis Vert_, and to that grand place where we see the head of the canal, of which he described the size and shape, and at the extremities of whose arms he placed the Trianon and the Menagerie. At each of the grand pieces whose position Le Nôtre marked, and whose future beauties he described, Louis XIV interrupted him, saying, 'Le Nôtre, I give you twenty thousand francs.' This magnificent approbation was so frequently repeated that it annoyed Le Nôtre, whose soul was as noble and disinterested as that of his master was generous. At the fourth interruption he stopped, and said brusquely to the King, 'Sire, Your Majesty shall hear no more. I shall ruin you.'"

In 1695 the King ennobled Le Nôtre and bestowed upon him the Order of St. Michael. Later, Le Nôtre presented to his sovereign his collection of pictures and bronzes, for which he had previously received an offer of 80,000 francs, or about $16,000. This collection was placed in one of the King's intimate rooms among the rarest objects in his possession. On occasion, when about to make a tour of the gardens, Louis liked to command a rolling chair similar to his own for the aged Le Nôtre. Discussing new projects, appraising those that were finished, they made the promenade together.

One of the first garden decorations undertaken was the Grotto of Thetis, a green alcove beautified by exquisite marbles and a fountain that stirred the muse of La Fontaine to sing. This graceful conceit, dominated by Apollo seated among the nymphs of Venus, was destroyed when Mansard built the north wing of the palace; the groups were removed to adorn other sites. While the vast pleasure-house was in course of construction, each year marked the creation of new fountains and woods. In 1664, the _Parterre du Nord_ was laid out below the windows of the north wing; in 1667 and 1668 the _Théâtre d'Eau_, the Maze, the Star, the Grand Canal, the Avenue of Waters, the Cascade of Diana and the Pyramid on the North Parterre, and the Green Carpet (_Tapis-Vert_) spread out in view of the windows of the rear facade of the palace. In 1670 and the three succeeding years the low-lying _Marais_ (fen) was constructed next to the Parterre of the Fountain of Latona, to meet the wishes of the King's favorite, Madame de Montespan. While she was in power "people spoke of the _Marais_ as one of the marvels of the gardens, but it was undoubtedly considered less wonderful after her fall," a writer comments. "In the center stood a large oak surounded by an artificial marsh, bordered with reeds and grasses, and containing plants and a number of white swans. From the swans, from the reeds and grasses, and from the leaves and branches of the oak, thousands of little jets of water leaped forth, falling like fine rain upon the masses of natural vegetation that flourished amid the artificial. At the sides of the bosquet there were two tables of marble, on which a collation was served when the marquise came to her grove to see the waters play. In 1704 the King ordered Mansard to destroy the _Marais_ and transform the bosquet into the Baths of Apollo."

In 1674 the Royal Isle came into being; and the next year the Arch of Triumph and the Three Fountains, between the Avenue of Waters and the château. In the thicket of the Three Fountains were "an immense number of small jets of water, leaping from basins at the sides and forming an arch of water overhead, beneath which one could walk without being wet. . . . The Arch of Triumph filled the end of the bosquet; it was placed on an estrade with marble steps, and was preceded by four lofty obelisks of gilded iron in which the water leaped and fell in sheets of crystal. The fountain itself was composed of three porticos of gilded iron, with large jets in the center of each, while seven jets leaped up from the basins above the porticos, and all the waters rushed down over the steps of marble. In addition, twenty-two vases at the sides of the bosquet threw jets into the air. 'Without having seen it,' says Blondel, 'it is impossible to imagine the wonderful effect produced by this decoration.'"

The Orangery was the chief work begun in 1678, and in the following year the superb Basin of Neptune and the Lake of the Swiss Guards were commenced. In the years 1680-1685 workmen were busy digging, laying pipes, planting and decorating the _Salle de Bal_, or outdoor salon of festivities, the Parterre of Fountains, and the Colonnade, where amid marble columns and balustrades the Court often came to sup and make merry.

In all, fourteen hundred gushing fountain jets animated the gardens. Le Nôtre, the author of these amazing water-works, died in the year 1700, when almost ninety years of age. Saint-Simon declared him justly renowned in that he had given to France gardens of so unique and ravishing a design that they completely outran in beauty the famous gardens of Italy. European landscape decorators counted it part of their education to journey to France for the purpose of studying the handiwork of the supreme craftsman.

An illustrated guide, printed at Amsterdam in 1682, contains the following quaint description of the Labyrinth, or Maze: "Courteous Reader," it begins, "it is sufficiently known how eminently France and especially the Royal Court doth excel above other places with all manner of delights. The admirable faire Buildings and Gardens with all imaginable ornaments and delightful spectacles represent to the eye of the beholder such abundant and rich objects as verily to ravish the spectator. Amongst all these works there is nothing more admirable and praiseworthy than the Royal Garden at Versailles, and, in it, the Labyrinth. Other representations are commonly esteemed because they please the eye, but this because it not only delights the ear and eye, but also instructs and edifies. This Labyrinth is situated in a wood so pleasant that Daedalus himself would have stood amazed to behold it. The Turnings and Windings, edged on both sides with green cropt hedges, are not at all tedious, by reason that at every hand there are figures and water-works representing the mysterious and instructive fables of Aesop, with an explanation of what Fable each Fountain representeth carved on each in black marble. Among all the Groves in the Park at Versailles the Labyrinth is the most to be recommended, as well for the novelty of the design as the number and diversity of the fountains that with ingenuity and _naïveté_ express the philosophies, of the sage Aesop. The animals of colored bronze are so modeled that they seem truly to be in action. And the streams of water that come from their mouths may be imagined as bearing the words of the fable they represent. There are a great number of fountains, forty in all, each different in subject, and of a style of decoration that blends with the surrounding verdure. At the entrance to the Maze is a bronze statue of Aesop himself--the famous Mythologist of Phrygia."

[Illustration: The Fountain of Versailles]

To appreciate the engineering skill of the directors of fountain construction at Versailles it must be remembered that it was from an arid plateau that hundreds of streams were made to spring from the earth. Thousands of laborers were employed to lay beneath the surface of the ground a net-work of canals and aqueducts to receive the tribute of water-courses directed hither from distant sources. The waters were finally pumped into immense reservoirs adroitly dissembled on the roofs of buildings overlooking the park. From these tanks a maze of pipes carried the water to thickets, grottoes, basins, fountains and canals. Nothing could surpass the ingenuity with which all this was contrived. The play of water directed to the Basin of the Mirrors reappeared later in the Baths of Apollo and the Fountain of the Dragon. Flowing in turn among successive pools and ornamental groups-- branching hither and yon in the gardens, the stream attained its full display in the most majestic effect of all, the Basin of Neptune.

"Here again is the hand of Le Nôtre," remarks James Farmer, author of "Versailles and the Court Under Louis XIV." "The basin of Neptune, called at first the Grand Cascades, was constructed from 1679 to 1684, in accordance with his designs. This immense basin, surrounded on the side toward the chateau by a handsome wall of stone, and on the other by an amphitheater of turf and trees,--a vast half-circle, in the center of which stands a marble statue of Renown, is simple in conception and imposing from its size. The richly carved lead vases which adorn the wall were gilded under the Grand Monarch, and each throws a jet of water to a great height. Dangeau tells us that His Majesty saw the waters play here for the first time on the 17th of May, 1685, and that he was quite content. However, Neptune had not then appeared in the basin that now bears his name; for the large groups of Neptune, the Ocean, and the Tritons, which ornament the base of the wall at present, were not put in place until 1739, in the reign of Louis XV. This majestic basin at the foot of the _Allée d'Eau_ is a striking contrast to Perrault's ugly Pyramid at the head of it. Le Nôtre knew what was fitting for the gardens of a Sun King."

A vast avenue, interrupted by many fair reaches of water, stretched its level length before the windows of the Grand Gallery. It was prolonged to the outer bounds of the gardens by the Grand Canal, on whose gleaming surface the sky was mirrored in the dusk of dawn, the golden glow of noon, or the sunset of declining day. This has ever been the supreme view from the palace of Versailles. Standing at one of the great windows of the Hall of Mirrors, the _Galerie des Glaces_, it often pleased the ruler of France to admire the Fountain of Latona, casting its fifty jets of water from the circular pool below the twin terraces. Beyond, the Green Carpet glowed in its emerald beauty among the clear waters of Versailles. The furthest fountain that met the eye was the Basin of Apollo, with its plunging bronze horses. In the outer park, that held the Trianon and the Menagerie, the royal gaze beheld the cross-shaped Canal which so often, in the revels that marked the first part of this reign, bore gay Venetian barges between the scintillating lights and fireworks that illumined the shore. At the right side, still looking from the rear of the chateau, the King's beauty-loving eyes dwelt upon the North Terrace, with its rich growth of greenery, on the graceful Fountains of the Pyramid and the Dragon, and above all on the magnificently soaring fountains of Neptune's Basin. At his left were the Terrace of Flowers, the two stairways that flanked the Orangery, chief work of Mansard and especial pride of Louis, and the lake in the small park named for the Swiss Guards. Nowhere, it is safe to say, could a place be found that embraced so many beautiful garden views at one time.

Bordering the avenue that Le Nôtre opened through the primitive groves where Louis XIII once came to hunt--on either side the broad lane of trees and leaping waters--groves were laid out, varied in design and decoration-- delectable retreats where lovers, traitors, diplomats might vow and plot, beneath the discreet ears of marble nymphs and goddesses.

Many of the groups and marble figures that beautified the walks and bowers of Versailles were conceived by the gifted Lebrun. Among his designs were the Four Seasons, the Four Quarters of the Globe, the Four Kinds of Poetry (Heroic, Satiric, Lyric and Pastoral), the Four Periods of the Day (Morning, Noon, Twilight, Night), the Four Elements (Earth, Air, Fire, Water), the Four Temperaments (Phlegmatic, Melancholy, Coleric and Sanguine). Mythological figures, vases ornamented with bas-reliefs of Louis XIV and great men of his reign, fountain groups representing the chief rivers of France, water nymphs, sportive babies, beasts in combat--sculpture massive, graceful, grotesque--all added their individual lure to the dells, the walks and the terraces of the magic palace.

Tile-workers from Flanders, marble-cutters from the Pyrenees, Italy and Greece, masons, sculptors, castmen, metal-workers, bronze colorists--innumerable artisans trained to meet the exacting tastes of that Silver Age of Art--lent their skill to the construction of fountains whose ingenuity and variety have set a standard for all time for the makers of kingly estates. A hundred sculptors of highest reputation were engaged to model groups, statues, busts and low reliefs for the Versailles park, under the supervision of Lebrun and Mignard.

Ladies of the Court sometimes claimed the ear of the compliant André Le Nôtre to suggest fancies that he graciously evolved with greenery and marbles, with tinkling streams and bright-winged birds.

The new Orangery, begun by Mansard on plans submitted by Le Nôtre, consumed nearly ten years in building, from 1678 to 1687. Twin stairways, one hundred and three steps high, united the South Parterre with the Parterre of the Orangery. The shelter erected for the protection of hundreds of orange trees, which often blossomed and came to fruit, contained a main gallery and two lateral galleries, lighted by twelve large windows. In the center stood a huge statue of Louis the Great. During warm weather the tubs containing the orange trees were set out on the Orange Parterre between the lofty stone stairways. The Orangery was one of the favorite retreats of the King. Besides the royal family, only those were permitted to stroll among the fragrant trees that had been granted special permission to do so.

It was in 1688, after more than a quarter of a century's labor, the sacrifice of hundreds of lives, and the expenditure of over fifty million francs, that the splendid parks and gardens with their buildings and fountains were finally achieved. Le Nôtre's successors rearranged some of the fountains and groves; others were renamed. In 1739-1740 there were placed near the Basin of Neptune three groups that still lend adornment to this spot. This was the final attempt to decorate the gardens during the reign of the House of the Bourbons. Strangers from every clime marveled at the beauty of the fountains. The ambassadors from the Court of Siam were astounded "that so much of bronze, marble and gilded metal could find place in a single garden." A member of the train of the Ambassador from England described the park, in 1698, as "a whole province traced by avenues, paths, canals, and ornamented in all ways possible by masterpieces of ancient and modern art."

The avenues were of white sand, with grassy by-ways on either side bordered by elms and iron railings six or seven feet high. Beyond these were thickets and niches where statues, sculptured urns and benches of white carved stone were placed. Occasional archways of green led down dim arbors to new enchantments. Here and there were round or star-shaped retreats whose carpets of grass were sprayed by murmuring fountains. In each recess were marble pedestals, busts, a long bench that invited repose.

Trees of mature growth were brought in great numbers from distant parts of France and Flanders. Despite difficulties of transportation, twenty-five thousand trees were carried on wagons from Artois alone. The forests of Normandy were denuded of yew-trees; from the mountains of _Dauphiné_ the King's emissaries brought _epicea_ trees, and India sent chestnut trees for the adornment of Versailles.

Among these groves Louis delighted to promenade in the evening, sometimes, in the _belle saison_, until midnight. Often he went on foot, but oftener in a light carriage drawn by a team of small black horses that had been given him by the Duke of Tuscany.

THE GRAND TRIANON

This palace decorated with pilasters of pink marble was not the first building chosen by the Grand Monarch to occupy the site at the end of the north arm of the canal of Versailles. Ambitious to extend his domain, the King had purchased and razed a shabby little village named Trianon, and on its somewhat dreary site erected for Madame de Montespan a villa so unpretentious as to arouse the comment of courtiers accustomed to the ruler's profligacy at Versailles. The vases of faïence that shone among the figures of gilded lead, the walk ornamented with Dutch tiles, the cornices of blue and white stucco, in the Chinese fashion, gave the little house the name, the Porcelain Trianon. Poets called it the Palace of Flora because of the wondrous gardens where rare flowers perfumed the pleasaunce in summer. Built in 1670, probably on designs of Francois Le Vau, the Porcelain Trianon was demolished toward the end of the year 1686.

There remains to-day nothing to remind us of the Villa of Flowers but the gardens and a fountain for horses near the canal, where a terrace planted with beautiful trees overlooks it. Here Louis XIV often came in a gondola on summer evenings, when the Marble Trianon had replaced the Trianon of Porcelain. The latter's demolition was inspired, no doubt, by the urging of the new favorite, Madame de Maintenon, who found distasteful this reminder of another's supremacy in the King's affections.

Moreover, this site continued to please the King for he recognized its convenience to the palace, and its accessibility by barge or carriage. He determined to build in the midst of these enchanting woods and blooms a dwelling less formal than the one at Versailles, smaller even than the one at Marly, but more habitable than the porcelain _maisonette_--a retreat, in short, where, without wearisome ceremony, he could retire with certain favored ones of his Court and while the summer hours away.

The accounts of the King's treasurer show that the building of the edifice and the gardens proceeded rapidly during the year 1687. By the end of November the royal master found his new residence "well advanced and very beautiful." Soon after the New Year he heard the opera "Roland" performed here, and was pleased to dine for the first time within the new walls. He gave orders on recurring visits for the embellishment of the summer palace. The Trianon of marble and porphyry, "the most graceful production of Mansard," was finally completed in the autumn of 1688. But the work of decoration went on under the hands of a horde of artists almost until the end of the monarch's reign.

Says an English author of a century ago: "In the midst of all the austerities imposed upon him by the ambition of Madame de Maintenon, the King went to Trianon to inhale the breath of the flowers which he had planted there, of the rarest and most odoriferous kind. On the infrequent occasions when the Court was permitted to accompany him thither to share in his evening collation, it was a beautiful spectacle to see so many charming women wandering in the midst of the flowers on the terrace rising from the banks of the canal. The air was so rich with the mingled perfume of violets, orange flowers, jessamines, tuberoses, hyacinths and narcissuses that the King and his visitors were sometimes obliged to fly from the overpowering sweets. The flowers in the parterres were arranged in a thousand different figures, which were constantly changed, so that one might have supposed it to be the work of some fairy, who, passing over the gardens, threw upon them each time a new robe aglow with color."

In the salons and copses where Louis the Great basked in the somewhat chary smiles of his latest (and last) favorite, his grandson, the fifteenth of his name, was to install the fascinating Madame de Pompadour. The very apartments once dedicated to the use of Madame de Maintenon, and later to Queen Marie Leczinska, became the living-rooms of the reigning mistress of the heart of Louis XV.

The Revolution spared the Grand Trianon. But under pretext of restoring it and rendering it, according to their tastes, more habitable, Napoleon First and Louis Philippe spared it less. The last king of France commanded in 1836 the architectural changes necessary to convert the Trianon into the royal residence, in place of the chateau of Versailles. He stayed here for the last time in the winter of 1848, before departing for Dreux. But, despite changes and mutilations, the facade and the interior of the rose-colored palace retain the stamp of the Great King who sponsored the Gallery of Mirrors, the Antechamber of the Bull's Eye, and the Chapel at Versailles.

CHAPTER V
A DAY WITH THE SUN KING

Louis the Magnificent, we must agree with that profuse and sharp-witted chronicler, the Duke of Saint-Simon, was made for a brilliant Court. "In the midst of other men, his figure, his courage, his grace, his beauty, his grand mien, even the tone of his voice and the majestic and natural charm of all his person, distinguished him till his death as the King Bee, and showed that if he had been born only a simple private gentleman, he would have excelled in fetes, pleasures and gallantry. . . . He liked splendor, magnificence and profusion in everything. Nobody ever approached his magnificence."

With sumptuous detail the King's day progressed at Versailles, from the formal "rising" to the hour when, with equal pomp, the monarch went to bed. Before eight o'clock in the morning the waiting-room next the King's bedchamber was the gathering-place of princes, nobles and officers of the Court, each fresh from his own laving and be-wigging. While they passed the time in low converse, the formal ceremony of the King's awakening took place behind the gold and white doors of the royal sleeping-room. "The Chamber," one of the eleven offices in the service of the King, comprised four first gentlemen of the Chamber, twenty-four gentlemen of the Chamber, twenty-four pages of the Chamber, four first valets of the Chamber, sixteen ushers, thirty-two valets of the Chamber, two cloak-bearers, two gun-bearers, eight barbers, three watch-makers, one dentist, and many minor attendants--all under the direction of the Grand Chamberlain.

A few minutes before eight o'clock it was the duty of the chief _valet de chambre_ to see that a fire was laid in the King's chamber (if the weather required one), that blinds were drawn, and candles snuffed. As the clock chimed the hour of eight, he approached the embroidered red velvet curtains of the royal bed with the announcement, "Sire, it is the hour."

When the curtains were drawn and the royal eyelids lifted upon a new day, the children of the King were admitted to make their morning obeisance. The chief physician and surgeon and the King's old nurse then entered to greet the waking monarch. While they performed certain offices allotted them, the Grand Chamberlain was summoned. The first _valet de chambre_ took his place by the bed and, holding a silver basin beneath the King's hands, poured on them spirits of wine from a flagon. The Grand Chamberlain next presented the vase of Holy Water to the King, who accepted it and made the Sign of the Cross. Opportunity was given at this moment for the princes, or any one having the _grande entrée_, to speak to the King, after which the Grand Chamberlain offered to His Majesty a prayer-book, and all present passed from the room except those privileged to stay for the brief religious service that followed.

Surrounded by princes, nobles and high officers attached to his person, the King chose his wig for the day, put on the slippers and dressing-gown presented by the appointed attendant, and stepped outside the massive balustrade that surrounded his bed. Now the doors opened to admit those that had the right to be present while the King donned his silk stockings and diamond-buckled garters and shoes--acts that he performed "with address and grace." On alternate days, when his night-cap had been removed, the nobles and courtiers were privileged to see the King shave himself, while a mirror, and, if the morning was dull, lighted candles were held before his face by the first _valet de chambre_. Occasionally His Majesty briefly addressed some one in the room. The assemblage was, by this time, augmented by the admission of secretaries and officers attached to the palace, whose position entitled them to the "first _entrée_." When his wig was in place and the dressing of the royal person had proceeded at the hands of officers of the Wardrobe (there were, in all, sixty persons attached to this service), the King spoke the word that opened the ante-chamber doors to the cardinals, ambassadors and government officials that awaited the ceremony of the _grand lever_, or "grand rising," so-called in distinction to the more intimate _petit lever_. Altogether, no less than one hundred and fifty persons were present while the King went through the daily ceremony of the rising and the toilet.

When the Sovereign of France had breakfasted on a service of porcelain and gold, had permitted his sword and his jeweled orders to be fastened on, and, from proffered baskets of cravats and handkerchiefs, had made his choice; when he had prayed by his bedside with cardinals and clergy in attendance; had granted brief informal interviews, and had attended mass in the chapel of Versailles, it was his custom to ask for the Council. Thrice a week there was a council of State, and twice a week a finance council. Thus the mornings passed, with the exception of Thursday morning, when His Majesty gave "back-stair" audiences known to but a few, and Friday morning, which was spent with his confessor.

Louis was always a busy man of affairs and never shirked his kingly duties. It was a principle of his life to place duty first and pleasure after. He told his son in his memoirs that an idle king showed ingratitude toward God and injustice toward man. "The requirements and demands of royalty," he wrote, "which may, at times, appear hard and irksome, you should find easy and agreeable in high places. Nothing will exhaust you more than idleness. If you tire of great affairs, and give up to pleasures, you will soon be disgusted with your own idleness. To take in the whole world with intelligent eyes, to be learning constantly what is going on in the provinces and among other nations--the court secrets, the habits, the weaknesses of princes and foreign ministers, to see clearly what all people are trying, to their utmost, to conceal, to fathom the most deep-seated thoughts and convictions of those that attend us in our own court--what greater pleasure and satisfaction could there be, if we were simply prompted by curiosity?"

Ordinarily, when at Versailles, the King dined alone at one o'clock, seated by the middle window of his chamber, overlooking the courtyards, the Place d'Armes, and the long avenue that led to Paris. More than three hundred persons,--stewards, chefs, butlers, gentlemen servants, carvers, cup-bearers, table-setters, cellarers, gardeners,--were charged with the care of the kitchens, pantries, cellars, fruit-lofts, store-rooms, linen closets, and treasuries of gold and silver plate belonging to the King's immediate household--the _Maison du Roi_. The Officers of the Goblet were present when the King was served, having first, with attendant ceremonies, "made the trial" of napkins and table implements as a safeguard from evil designs against his life. Even the simplest repast served to the King comprised many dishes, for the Grand Monarch ate heartily, though with discriminating appetite.

Unless the Sovereign dined in the privacy of his bed-chamber, he was surrounded by princes and courtiers. At "public dinners" a procession of well-dressed persons continually passed through the room to observe the King at his dining.

It was ordained that the King's meat should be brought to the table from the kitchens in the Grand Commune after this manner: "Two of His Majesty's guards will march first, followed by the usher of the hall, the _maître d'hôtel_ with his baton, the gentleman servant of the pantry, the controller-general, the controller clerk of the Office, and others who carry the Meat, the equerry of the kitchen and the guard of the plates and dishes, and behind them two other guards of His Majesty, who are to allow no one to approach the Meat.

"In the Office called the _Bouche_, the equerry of the Kitchen arranges the dishes upon a table, and presents two trials of bread to the _maître d'hôtel_, who makes the trial of the first course, and who, having placed the meats for the trial upon these two trials of bread, gives one to the equerry of the Kitchen, who eats it, while the other is eaten by the _maître d'hôtel_. Afterward the gentleman servant takes the first dish, the second is taken by the controller, and the other officers of the Kitchen take the rest. They advance in this order: the _maître d'hôtel_, having his baton, marches at the head, preceded some steps by the usher of the hall, carrying his wand, which is the sign of his office, and in the evening bearing a torch as well. When the Meat, accompanied by three of the body-guards with carbines on their shoulders, has arrived (that is, in the first antechamber, where the King is to dine), the _maître d'hôtel_ makes a reverence to the _nef_. The gentleman servant, holding the first dish, places it upon the table where the _nef_ is, and having received a trial portion from the gentleman servant in charge of the trial table, he makes the trial himself and places his dish upon the trial table. The gentleman servant having charge of this table takes the other dishes from the hands of those who carry them, and places them also on the trial table. After the trial of them has been made they are carried by the other gentlemen servants to the table of the King.

"The first course being on the table, the _maître d'hôtel_ with his baton, preceded by the usher of the hall with his wand, goes to inform the King; and when His Majesty has arrived at table the _maître d'hôtel_ presents a wet napkin to him, of which trial has been made in the presence of the officer of the Goblet, and takes it again from the King's hands. During the dinner the gentleman servant in charge of the trial table continues to make trial in the presence of the officers of the Goblet and of the Kitchen of all that they bring for each course.

"When His Majesty desires to drink, the cup-hearer cries at once in a loud tone, 'The drink for the King!' makes a reverence to the King, and goes to the sideboard to take from the hands of the chief of the Wine-cellars the salver and cup of gold, and the two crystal decanters of wine and water. He returns, preceded by the chiefs of the Goblet and the Wine-cellars, and the three, having reached the King's table, make a reverence to His Majesty. The chief of the Goblet, standing near the King, holds a little trial cup of silver-gilt, into which a gentleman servant pours a small quantity of wine and water from the decanters. A portion of this the chief of the Goblet pours into a second trial cup which is presented by his assistant, who, in turn, hands it to the gentleman servant. The chief and the gentleman servant make the trial, and when the latter has handed his cup to the chief, that officer returns both cups to his assistant. When the trial has been made in this manner in the King's sight, the gentleman servant, making a reverence to the King, presents to His Majesty the cup of gold and the golden salver on which are the decanters. The King pours out the wine and water, and having drunk, replaces the cup upon the salver. The gentleman servant makes another reverence to the King, and returns the salver and all upon it to the chief of the Wine-cellars, who carried it to the side-board."

The ceremony of tasting the King's wine was most impressive, and it was regarded as a necessary and effective safeguard against poisonous attacks or deleterious effects on His Majesty's august health. The thought is suggested, however, that the test could have been effective only in case of immediate or quick-working poison. A slow and insidious drug--and there were experts in such concoctions in those days--would surely have passed the taster's test and affected the King in time. The test was but a mere formality, however, for Louis was the Most Adored Monarch. As one chronicler has observed, "He was not only majestic, he was amiable. Those that surrounded him, the members of his family, his ministers, his domestics, loved him." Poison played no part in his career. That subtle method of attack was reserved for Louis XVI and Marie Antoinette, on both of whom it was attempted more than once.

The carver, having taken his place before the table of the King, presented and uncovered all the dishes, and when His Majesty told him to do so, or made him a sign, he removed them, handing them to the plate-changer or to his assistants. He changed the King's plate and napkin from time to time, and cut the meats when the King did not cut them himself.

On rare occasions, when the King was in residence at Versailles, his brother dined with him. But large, formal dinners were rare, and women were seldom at the King's table except on grand occasions.

Upon leaving the table, Saint-Simon tells us, "the King immediately entered his cabinet. That was the time for distinguished people to speak to him. He stopped at the door a moment to listen, then entered; very rarely did any one follow him, never without asking permission to do so; and for this few had the courage.... The King amused himself by feeding his dogs, and remained with them more or less time, then asked for his wardrobe, changed before the very few distinguished people it pleased the first gentleman of the Chamber to admit there, and immediately went out by the back stairs into the court of marble to get the air.... He went out for three objects: stag-hunting, once or more each week; shooting in his parks (and no man handled a gun with more grace or skill), once or twice each week; and walking in his gardens, and to see his workmen."

The King was fond of hunting and the chase held an important part in the service of the royal household. The conditions of the sport were determined with a formality in keeping with the other affairs of Versailles. There were two divisions of the chase--the hunting and the shooting. The first had to do with the chase of the stag, deer, wild boar, wolf, fox and the hare. The shooting had to do with smaller game. Here was also falconry, though in this Louis was not particularly interested. The chase was conducted by the Grand Huntsman of France, and his duties were enormous and varied. Under him the Captain General of the Toils kept the woods of Versailles well stocked with stag, deer, boars, and other animals caught in the forests of France. Some idea of the pomp and ceremony of the hunt may be obtained from the following account which was printed in the _Mercure Galant_ in 1707:

"The toils were placed in the glades of Bombon. In the inclosure there were a large number of stags, wild boars, roebucks, and foxes. The court arrived there. The King, the Queen of England (the wife of James II, then in exile), her son, Madame la Duchesse de Bourgogne, and Madame (the Duchesse d'Orleans, wife of Monsieur) were in the same carriage, and all the princesses and the ladies followed in the carriages and _calèches_ of the king. A very large number of noblemen on horseback accompanied the carriages. Within the inclosure there were platforms, arranged with seats covered with tapestry for the ladies, and many riding-horses for the nobles who wished to attack the game with swords or darts. They killed sixteen of the largest beasts, and some foxes. Mgr. le Duc de Berry slew several. This chase gave much pleasure on account of the brilliancy of the spectacle, and the large number of nobles who surrounded the toils. A multitude of people had climbed into the trees, and by their diversity they formed an admirable background."

Stag hunting was even more impressive in ceremonial details. After the chase the "quarry" was usually held by torchlight at Versailles, in one of the inner courts, and the ceremony of the quarry was as follows: "When His Majesty had made known his intentions on the subject, all the huntsmen with their horns and in hunting-dress came to the place where the quarry was to be made. On the arrival of the King, who was also in hunting-dress, the grand huntsman, who had received two wands of office, gave one to the King, and retained the other. The dogs were held under the whip about the carcass of the stag until the grand huntsman, having received the order from the King, gave the sign with his wand that they should be set at liberty. The horns sounded, and the huntsmen, who while the hounds were held under the whip had cried, 'Back, dogs! Back!' shouted now, 'Hallali, valets! Hallali!' When the quarry had been made, that is to say, when the flesh had been torn from the bones, a valet took the _forhu_ (the belly of the stag, washed and placed on the end of a forked stick), and called the dogs, crying, '_Tayaut, tayaut_!' and threw the _forhu_ into the midst of the pack, where it was devoured at once. At this instant the fanfares redoubled, and finished by sounding the retreat. The King returned the wand to the grand huntsman, who at the head of all the huntsmen followed His Majesty."

In his promenades at Versailles and Trianon any courtiers that chose to do so were permitted to follow the King. On his return from out-door recreation His Majesty, after again changing his costume, remained in his cabinet resting or working. Frequently he passed some time in the apartments of Madame de Maintenon.

At ten o'clock the captain of the guard announced supper in the chamber between the Hall of the King's Guards and the antechamber called "Bull's Eye." This meal was always on a pretentious scale, and was attended at table by the royal children and numerous courtiers and ladies. When the last course had been served the King retired to his bedchamber and there for a few moments received all his Court, before passing into his Cabinet, where he spent something less than an hour in the company of his immediate household, his brother seated in an arm-chair, the princesses upon stools, and the Dauphin and all the other princes standing.

When the King had bid the company goodnight he entered his sleeping-room, where were already the courtiers privileged to attend the ceremony of the _coucher_, or going-to-bed. At the _grand coucher_ the King, being formally divested of his hat, gloves, cane and sword, knelt by the balustrade about his bed, while an almoner murmured a prayer as he held a lighted candle above the royal head. When the King had risen from his knees he gave to the first _valet de chambre_ his watch and the holy relics he was accustomed to wear, and proceeded through the assemblage to his chair. This was the moment when, with regal mien, the Sun King bestowed the candle upon whomever he wished to honor--a ceremony brief, trifling, but significant of the Monarch of Monarchs in its gracious portent.

To the Master of the Wardrobe fell the task of removing the King's coat and vest; the diamond buckles of the right and left garters were unfastened respectively by the first _valet de chambre_ and the first valet of the wardrobe, and the valets of the Chamber withdrew with the kingly shoes and breeches while the pages of the Chamber presented slippers and dressing-gown. The latter was held as a screen while the shirt was removed, and the night-dress was accepted from the hands of a royal prince, or the Grand Chamberlain.

Having put on the dressing-gown, the King, with an inclination of the head, dismissed the courtiers, to whom the ushers cried, "Gentlemen, pass on!"

All those that were entitled to remain for the _petit coucher_--princes, clergymen, officers, chosen intimates--then disposed themselves about the bedchamber while the King submitted to the hands of his coiffeur and received from the Grand Master of the Wardrobe the night-cap and handkerchiefs. After bathing his face and hands in a silver basin held by a royal prince or grand master, the _petit coucher_ was at an end. The bathing apartments of Versailles were numerous and luxuriously appointed, but, though the most trivial details in the daily life of His Majesty were attended with imposing circumstance, there is no record of a Ceremony of the King's Bath, nor do we know of any noble order at the Grand Monarch's court that held the title of Knights of the Bath.

When the assemblage that witnessed the _petit coucher_ in the royal apartment had dwindled one by one, according to precedent, the Master of Versailles was, at last, free to do as he chose,--to play with his dogs in an adjoining cabinet, or take his ease in pleasing solitude. Then, in the familiar words of Samuel Pepys' immortal diary, "Home, and to bed." Outside the gilded balustrade the first _valet de chambre_ slept on a folding cot. "Beyond that balustrade, by the faint candle-light, there loomed among the shadows a white-plumed canopy and crimson curtains. The Grand Monarch slept."

CHAPTER VI
GOLDEN DAYS AND RED LETTER NIGHTS

The Gayety and Fashion of Versailles Life. The Prodigal Frivolities and Diversions of the Court.

The ceremonious routine of the days at Versailles was enlivened at certain times of the year by festivities of astounding brilliance, and, on occasion, by gorgeous receptions offered to visiting rulers and ambassadors, It has already been related that the arrival of Louis XIV and his family at Versailles in the fall of 1663 was celebrated by a fete at which a troupe headed by Molière was heard in a piece by the great dramatist called Impromptu de Versailles, In the month of May, 1664, Louis commanded a performance of "Pleasures of the Enchanted Isle," in which his favorite actor and playwright furnished the comedy, Lully the music and the ballets, and an Italian mechanician the decorations and illuminations. On the first day there was tilting at the ring, in which pastime Louis XIV played a part, wearing a diamond-embroidered costume. The next day, on an outdoor stage, Molière and his company played the "_Princesse d'Élide_." There followed ballets, races, tourneys and a lottery, "in which the prizes were pieces of furniture, silverware and precious stones."

In September, 1665, a hunt was organized in the woods of Versailles, at which the royal ladies wore Amazonian habits. A mid-winter day in the year 1667 was chosen for a tournament "that over-passed the limits of magnificence." The Queen herself led a cortege of Court beauties on a white horse that was set off by brocaded and gem-sewn trappings. The _Gazette_ of 1667 described the appearance of the youthful Master of Versailles at this tournament, he being "not less easily recognized by the lofty mien peculiar to him than by his rich Hungarian habit covered with gold and precious stones, his helmet with waving plumes, his horse that was arrayed in magnificent accouterments and a jeweled saddle-cloth."

Again in the summers of 1668 and 1672 Molière and Lully entertained the guests at the King's chateau, while in the gardens there were statues, vases and chandeliers so lighted as to give the impression that they glowed with interior names.

In the summer of 1674, Molière "was no longer alive to arrange dramatic performances among the green and flowery coppices of Versailles. But there was no lack of entertainment at the splendid fêtes that marked that year. We have the recital of Félebien, a fastidious chronicler of Court doings, referring to this period of merry-making, which lasted during most of the summer and fall.

"The King," says Félebien, "ordained as soon as he arrived at Versailles that festivities be arranged at once, and that, at intervals, new diversions should be prepared for the pleasure of the Court. The things most noticeable at such times as these were the promptitude, minute pains and silent ease with which the King's orders were invariably executed. Like a miracle--all in a moment--theaters rose, wooded places were made gay with fountains, collations were spread, and a thousand other things were accomplished that one would have supposed would require a long time and a vast bustle of workers."

The "Grand Fêtes" occupied six days of the months of July and August. The celebrations of the fourth of July began with a feast laid on the verdant site later usurped by the basin called the Baths of Apollo. Here the beauty of nature was enhanced by an infinity of ornate vases filled with garlands of flowers. Fruits of every clime were served on platters of porcelain, in silver baskets and in bowls of priceless glass. In the evening the Court attended a production of _"Alceste"_--an opera by Quinault and Lully, executed by artists from the Royal Academy of Music. The stage was set in the Marble Court. The windows facing the court were ablaze with two rows of candles. The walls of the chateau were screened with orange trees, festooned with flowers, illumined by candelabra made of silver and crystal. The marble fountain in the center of the court was surrounded by tall candlesticks and blossoming urns. The spraying waters escaped through vases of flowers, that their falling should not interrupt the voices of those on the stage. Artificial waters, silver-sconced tapers, bowers of fragrant shrubs united to create the richest of settings for this outdoor theater.

It was the King's wish that the grounds of the little "porcelain house" at Trianon be chosen as the scene of the second fête, which took place a week later. In an open-air enclosure, decorated by "a prodigious quantity of flowers," the guests listened to the "_Églogue de Versailles_," composed for the occasion by Lully, leader of the _Petits-Violons_, Louis' favorite Court orchestra. Afterwards all the nobles and their fair companions returned to sup at Versailles in a wood where the Basin of the Obelisk now is.

Seven days later, at the third fete of the series, the King gave a banquet to ladies in the pavilion at the Menagerie. The guests were conveyed in superbly decorated gondolas down the Grand Canal. In a large boat were violinists and hautboy-players that made sweet music. Finally, in a theater arranged this time before the Grotto, all the ladies were regaled with a performance of "_La Malade Imaginaire_," the last of Molière's comedies.

For the fourth festal day, the twenty-eighth of July, the King commanded a fête of surpassing beauty. The feast was laid in the center of the _Théâtre-d'Eau_. The steps forming the amphitheater served as tables for the arrangement of the viands. Orange trees heavy with blossoms and golden fruit, apple trees, apricot trees, trees laden with peaches, and tall oleanders--all set out in ornamental tubs; three hundred vessels of fine porcelain filled with fruit; one hundred and twenty baskets of dried preserves; four hundred crystal cups containing ices, an uncounted number of carafes sparkling with rare liqueurs--all created a picture of colorful luxury, which, we are assured, struck those that looked upon it as "most agreeable." Threading their musical murmurings through all the laughter and badinage, the tossing jets of the pyramidal fountains fell away to pools and green-bordered streams.

Lully's opera, "_Cadmus et Hermione_," Was sung in a theater arranged at the end of the Allée of the Dragon. At its close every one made a tour of the park in open vehicles, lighted by torches carried by lackeys, and all assisted at an exhibition of fire-works on the canal. The evening ended with a supper in the Marble Court. Here an illuminated column was placed on an immense pedestal, while around it was disposed a table with seats for fifty persons.

The fifth gala day was marked by the presentation to the King of one hundred and seven flags and standards that Condé, the illustrious general, had taken at the battle of Senef. In the evening the company toured the park of Versailles, occupying thirty six-horse carriages. After a supper served in a forest retreat the invited ones witnessed a performance of "Iphigénie," a new tragedy by Racine, which was most admirably played by the royal troupe, and much applauded by the Court. There followed a grand illumination of the great fountain at the head of the canal--a display whose beauty and ingenuity "surprised every one"--even the luxury-surfeited guests of Versailles. Besides an encircling balustrade six feet in height and ornamented with _fleurs de lys_ and the arms of the King (all of which glowed with a golden light most lovely to look upon), there were high pedestals that appeared to be of transparent marble, with ornaments representing Apollo and the Sun, whose device Louis, instigator of all the splendor of Versailles, had adopted as his own insignia. These decorations were made after designs by Lebrun.

On the night of the thirty-first of August, the sixth and last day of the fêtes, the Court witnessed what seemed to be indeed a magic spectacle. "His Majesty," it is recorded, "coming out of the château at one o'clock in the morning, beneath a starless sky, suddenly beheld about him a miraculous rain of lights. All the parterres glittered. The grand terrace in front of the château was bordered by a double row of lights. The steps and railings of the horseshoe, all the walls, all the fountains, all the reservoirs, shone with myriad flames. The borders of the Grand Canal were adorned with statues and architectural decorations, behind which lights had been placed to make them transparent. The King, the Queen, and all the Court took their seats in richly ornamented gondolas. Boats filled with musicians followed them, and Echo repeated the sounds of an enchanted harmony."

Thus ended the fêtes of 1674--the last of their kind that were given by Louis XIV.

The Versailles calendar of events was divided into three periods: the season of the winter carnival, the pious observances of Easter, and the summer-time festivities. Ordinarily, in the winter months, there was a hunt on foot or horseback almost every day. In the warm season the Court often took part in a promenade by boat on the Grand Canal, followed by a concert and a feast for the ladies at Trianon or at the Menagerie. Ladies were always invited in great numbers to such parties. Sometimes they walked among the orange trees or made a tour of the gardens in light carriages, or repaired to the stables to watch the trainers putting the royal mounts through their paces. And always there were games of chance, for gambling was the ruling passion of the Court.

From the record of Dangeau we read a description of a gay tournament that took place in the riding-school of the Great Stables of Versailles on two successive June days:

"The King and Mme. la Dauphine (wife of the heir to the throne) dined at an early hour, and on leaving table, the King and Monseigneur entered a carriage. Mme. la Dauphine and many ladies followed in other carriages. In the court of the ministers, they found all the cavaliers of the tournament drawn up in two lines; the pages and lackeys were there also. Monseigneur mounted a horse at the head of one company; M. le Duc de Bourbon was at the head of the other. The King took his seat in the place prepared for him.

"The cavaliers first rode round the courtyard of the chateau, passing under the windows of the young Duc de Bourgogne (grandson of the King) who was on the balcony. Then they rode out of the gate and down the Avenue de Paris, and entered the riding-school of the Great Stables by a gate made near the Kennels. After riding in procession before the raised seats of the court, they took their posts, twenty cavaliers in each corner, with their pages and grooms behind them; the drums and trumpets at the barrier. The subject of the tournament was the Wars of Granada, and the cavaliers represented the Spaniards and the Moors. Monseigneur rode a tilt with the Due de Bourbon, and Messieurs de Vendôme and de Brionne rode at the same time to make the figure.... There were three courses run for the prize, which was won by the Prince de Lorraine. It was a sword ornamented with diamonds, and he received it from the hand of the King. After the tournament all the cavaliers conducted the King to the courtyard of the château, lance in hand, and the heads of the companies saluted him with their swords.

"On the fifth, a second tournament was held, and, in spite of the bad weather, the King found it more beautiful than the first. Many ladies were present. The Russian envoys, who had not seen the previous fête, occupied seats at the King's right. During a shower, the spectators retired quickly, but as soon as it had passed, all the seats were filled again. The Marquis de Plumartin won the prize. It was a sword adorned with diamonds, but more costly than that won by the Prince de Lorraine."

The Fête of Kings celebrated each year was a brilliant affair at Versailles. Then the Hall of Mirrors and Salons of War and Peace were illumined by hundreds upon hundreds of twinkling tapers, while over the floor glided a throng of slippered feet to the beat of strings and hautboys. At the suppers, which preceded and followed the dancing, seventy-two Swiss guards served the guests, each one distinguished by a ribbon corresponding with the color of the table to whose service he was assigned. It was the King's custom to retire from the revel with regal formalities at one hour after midnight. But the feasting and dancing continued many times until rosy dawn stole in the windows and paled the candle-light. Besides balls, concerts, plays, games of chance, masquerades, all the Court was invited every week--between October and Easter--to take part in the _appartements_ or receptions given by the King. These soirées began at seven o'clock and lasted till ten. The chief diversion was card-playing. The King, the Queen and all the princes so far unbent as to play with their guests at the same tables, and move about without ceremony, conversing, listening to the music of Lully's band, watching a minuet or a gavotte, eating and drinking, or bestowing special favors upon courtiers that engaged their momentary fancy.

Sometimes the losses of the players at the tables were enormous; again, nobles counted their gains by the hundred thousands. The youthful granddaughter of the King, the Duchess of Bourgogne, lost at one time a sum equaling 600,000 francs, which her doting grandfather paid, as he also paid debts of the Duke of Bourgogne. During one night's play the King himself lost a sum totaling "many millions." On occasion the courtiers were entertained at festivities arranged for the heir to the throne, or by the cardinal that was in residence at the chateau. During masked balls held in the carnival season dancers sometimes changed their costumes two or three times in an evening--one worn under another being revealed by pulling a silken cord. Often well-tempered confusion was caused by gay subterfuges--an exchange of masks, or the imposing of one mask on another. The costumes were sumptuous beyond words. "It is impossible to witness at one time more jewelry," naïvely recited the _Mercure_ in setting forth the richness of a _cercle_ at which the Court was present in 1707.

Let us read further from the _Mercure_ of the diversions that drove dull care away at a Court carnival: "There have been this winter five balls in five different apartments at Versailles, all so grand and so beautiful that no other royal house in the world can show the like. Entrance was given to masks only, and no persons presented themselves without being disguised, unless they were of very high rank.... People invent grotesque disguises, they revive old fashions, they choose the most ridiculous things, and seek to make them as amusing as possible.... Mgr. le Dauphin changed his disguise eight or ten times each evening. M. Bérain had need of all his wit to furnish these disguises, and of all his ingenuity to get them made up, since there was so little time between one ball and another. The prince did not wish to be recognized, and all sorts of extraordinary disguises were invented for him; frequently under the figures that concealed him, one could not have told whether the person thus masked was tall or short, fat or thin. Sometimes he had double masks, and under the first a mask of wax so well made that, when he took off his first mask, people fancied they saw the natural face, and he deceived everybody. Nothing can equal the enjoyment which Mgr. le Dauphin takes in all these diversions, nor the rapidity with which he changes his disguises. He leaves all his officers without being fatigued, although he works harder at dressing and undressing himself than they do, and he danced much. This prince shows in the least things, in his horsemanship, and in the ardor with which he follows the chase, what pleasure he will take some day in commanding armies. But could one expect less from the son of Louis the Great!

"The first of the five balls," continues the correspondent, "was given by M. le Grand, in his apartments in the new wing of Versailles. The ball commenced with a masquerade. They danced a minuet and a jig; but only Mlle. de Nantes danced in the latter. Mlle. de Nantes was especially admired when she danced, and made so great an impression that people stood on chairs to see her better, Mgr. le Dauphin came to the masquerade with M. le Prince de la Roche-sur-Yon and many other notables. He was in a sedan-chair, accompanied by a number of merry-andrews and dwarfs. He changed his disguise four or five times during the ball, which lasted until four o'clock in the morning.... The second ball was given by Mgr. le Dauphin in the hall of his Guards, which forms the entrance to his apartments. M. le Duc gave the third, which was magnificent. Some days after it was the turn of the Cardinal de Bouillon to receive the court."

"From just before Candlemas day to Easter of the year 1700," wrote Saint-Simon, "nothing was heard of but balls and pleasures of the Court. The

King gave at Versailles and Marly several masquerades, by which he was much amused under pretext of amusing the Duchesse de Bourgogne.

"No evening passed on which there was not a ball. The chancellor's wife gave one--which was a fête the most gallant and the most magnificent possible. There were different rooms for the fancy-dress ball, for the masqueraders, for a superb collation, for shops of all countries, Chinese, Japanese, etc., where many singular and beautiful things were sold, but no money taken; there were presents for the Duchesse de Bourgogne and the ladies. Everybody was especially diverted at this entertainment, which did not finish until eight o'clock in the morning. Madame de Saint-Simon and I passed the last three weeks of this time without ever seeing the day. Certain dancers were allowed to leave off dancing only at the same time as the Duchesse de Bourgogne. One morning, when I wished to escape too early, the duchesse caused me to be forbidden to pass the doors of the salon; several of us had the same fate. I was delighted when Ash Wednesday arrived, and I remained a day or two dead-beat."

The _Mercure_ describes the fête given by the wife of the Chancellor of France at her mansion beyond the palace grounds:

"Mme. la Duchesse de Bourgogne, learning that Mme. la Chancelière wished to give her a ball, received the proposition with much joy. Although there were but eight days in which to prepare for it, Mme. la Chancelière resolved to give the princess in one evening all the diversions that people usually take during all the carnival period--namely, comedy, fair, and ball. When the evening came, detachments of Swiss were posted in the street and in the courtyard, with many servants of Mme. la Chancelière, so that there was no confusion at the gates or in the court, which was brightly lighted with torches. . . . The ball-room was lighted by ten chandeliers and by magnificent gilded candelabra. At one end, on raised seats, were the musicians, hautboys and violins, in fancy dress with plumed caps. In front of the velvet-covered benches for the courtiers were three arm-chairs, one for Mme. la Duchesse de Bourgogne, and the others for Monsieur and the Madame. Beyond the ball-room, across the landing of the staircase, was another hall, brilliantly lighted, in which were hautboys and violins, and this hall was for the masks, who came in such numbers that the ball-room could not have contained them all.

". . . After remaining about an hour at the ball, Mme. la Chancelière and the Comte de Pontchartrain conducted Mme. la Duchesse de Bourgogne into another hall, filled with lights and mirrors, where a theater had been erected to furnish the diversion of a comedy. Only about one hundred people were allowed to enter the hall of comedy, and the princes and princesses of the blood, being masked, took no rank there. Mme. la Duchesse de Bourgogne and Madame had arm-chairs in the center of the hall. The Duchesse de Bourgogne was surprised to see a splendid theater, adorned with her arms and monogram.... As soon as the princess was seated, Bari, the famous mountebank of Paris, came forward and asked her protection against the doctors, and having extolled the excellence of his remedies, and the marvels of his secrets, he offered to the princess as a little diversion a comedy such as they sometimes played at Paris. There was given then a little comedy which Mme. le Chancelière had got M. Dancourt to write expressly for that fête. All the actors were from the company of the comedians of the king. They played to perfection, and received much praise.... At the end of the comedy, Mme. la Duchesse de Bourgogne was conducted into another hall, where a superb collation had been prepared in an ingenious manner. At one end of the hall, in a half-circle, were five booths, in which were merchants, clad in the costumes of different countries; a French pastry-cook, a seller of oranges and lemons, an Italian lemonade-seller, a seller of sweetmeats, a vendor of coffee, tea and chocolate. They were from the king's musicians, and sung their wares, accompanied by music, at the sides of the booths, and had pages to serve the guests. The booths were splendidly painted and gilded, adorned with lusters and flowers, and bore the arms and cipher of Mme. la Duchesse de Bourgogne. At the back of each booth a large mirror reflected the whole.... The Duchesse de Bourgogne left this hall, after the collation, delighted with all that she had seen and heard. Since the ball-room was so crowded with masks, the princess returned to the hall of comedy, where they held a smaller court ball until two o'clock, when she went to the grand ball to see the masks. She was much amused there until four in the morning. When Mme. la Chancelière and the Comte de Pontchartrain conducted her to the foot of the staircase, she thanked them much for the pleasure they had given her. This fete brought many congratulations to Mme. la Chancelière."

La Palatine, Duchess of Orleans, has left among her letters a description of her costume on a day of august ceremonies. "The crowd was so great," she wrote, "that we had to wait a quarter of an hour at the door of each salon before entering, and I was wearing a robe and an overskirt so intolerably heavy that I could scarcely stand erect. My costume was of gold woven with black chenille flowers, and my jewels were pearls and diamonds. Monsieur had on a coat of black velour embroidered with gold, and wore all his great diamonds. The coat of my son was embroidered with gold and a variety of other colors and it was covered with gems. The robe my daughter wore was made of green velour threaded with gold and garnished with rubies and diamonds. In her hair was an ornament designed in brilliants and sprays of rubies."

For these extraordinary functions the King and his entourage bedecked themselves with priceless ornaments. When in 1714 the Sun King received the ambassador of Siam, he chose a habit of black and gold bordered with diamonds, valued at 12,500,000 _livres_, or about $2,500,000. The weight was so great that he was compelled to change it soon after dinner. Besides the jewelry he wore on his own person, the royal host loaned for this event a garniture of diamonds and pearls to the Duke of Maine and another garniture of colored stones to the Count of Toulouse.

When the King of France received foreign ambassadors, or celebrated, with pomp befitting his tastes, marriages and births in the royal family, the Court, weightily, stiffly, sumptuously appareled, thronged through the Hall of Mirrors--the Grand Gallery--in spectacular defile.

These brilliant tableaux, the most brilliant of all Europe, had their source in the King's love of splendor and profusion. It was to please him that his courtiers and favorites staked fortunes at the gaming tables, outran each other in devising costly dresses, contrived novel equipages and unique dwellings. In his superb Court he found all the elements required to satisfy his pride, and glorify his reign. The Sun King was the most profligate host in all history. Determined to outdo the fabulous luxury of the feasts of Lucullus in early Roman times, and to outshine the storied splendor of Oriental princes, he entertained his Court and guests with lavish liberality, superbly indifferent to the cost of his boundless extravagance and considering not at all the day of reckoning that must come later for the Bourbon dynasty in France. To glow with commanding brilliance, like the Sun, in the center of his royal firmament, to overwhelm his subjects with his grandeur, and to dazzle the eyes of other nations--that was the ambition that Louis cherished and achieved.

CHAPTER VII
THE WOMEN OF VERSAILLES

We have pictured the Sun King and his imposing Court. We have told the story of the founding and construction of his luxurious palace, and described the spectacles and entertainments that made Versailles the most brilliant spot in Europe. We have said nothing of the women of Versailles and the part they played in the life of the Court and the influence they exerted in the affairs of France. Some of these women, though occupying the Queen's apartments and sharing the crown, lived an existence of bitter disappointment and thwarted affection--Queens in name only, and serving only as mothers of princes and future monarchs. Such were Marie Thérèse, the heart-sick wife of Louis XIV, and Marie Leczinska, the sad consort of Louis XV. About them were many brilliant women that graced the palace with their beauty and charm and made romantic court history that the chroniclers of the time fed on eagerly, and that the world has devoured eagerly ever since. Rich were those years in intrigue and adventure, and many and rapid were the changing fortunes of favorites. No one could tell what a day might bring forth. The woman of one hour might go the next. Self-interest stimulated the ambitious seekers of favors to constant endeavor. Grim, determined strugglers for social preference frequented the salons with smiling faces that sometimes glowed with pride and satisfaction, but more often veiled rankling disappointment and carking care.

Even the great Madame de Maintenon, who successfully weathered the storms of the social struggle for so many years, once exclaimed: "I can hold out no longer. I wish that I were dead." And a short time before her demise, she observed bitterly, "One atones in full for youthful joys and gratification. I can see, as I review my life, that since I was twenty-two years of age--when my good fortune began--I have not been free from suffering for a moment; and through my life my sufferings increased."

If Madame de Maintenon confessed so much in her last days, what must the other favorites of Versailles have experienced and felt? Each wore the mask of Comedy, with Tragedy gnawing beneath. These brilliant women, who seemed at times to be so happy, were little more than slaves, and we find them disclosed in the memoirs of the time as "penitents who make their apologies to history and lay bare to future generations their miseries, vexations and the remorse of their souls." The demands of Court life were constant and relentlessly exacting. The favorites, each one striving to outdo the others, knew not, from day to day, what way their destinies were leading them.

"If," exclaimed Saint-Amand, "among these favorites of the King, there were a single one that had enjoyed her shameful triumphs in peace, that could have recalled herself happy in the midst of her luxury and splendor, one might have concluded that, from a merely human point of view, it is possible to find happiness in vice. But no; there was not even one. The Duchesse de Châteauroux and Marquise de Pompadour were no happier than the Duchesse de la Vallière and the Marquise de Montespan."

The Sun King built Versailles and established his Court there. It was the women that made the life of Versailles--and gave their lives to it. The Court was a dazzling spider's web, and many a beautiful favorite became fatally entangled in its glittering meshes.

Louis XIV, when twenty-two years of age, married Marie Thérèse, daughter of Philip IV of Spain. If he had been a simple, respectable young man of France, he might then have settled down and finished the story by "living happily ever after." But he was not. He was the King of France; so he pursued the royal road that his antecedents had blazed before him; and the way was made easy and pleasant for him. In treading the "primrose path of dalliance" he allowed no grass to grow under his feet.

Louis made Marie Thérèse his Queen and consort in 1660, and it was only a year later when his fancy was caught by the dainty and attractive little Françoise Louise La Vallière. She was scarcely more than seventeen years of age when she became the favorite of the King. She was a delicate little creature, slightly lame, but most feminine in her appeal, and she caught the King by her very girlishness, as she played like a child with him in the parks of the palace. She was a simple maid of honor to Queen Marie Thérèse when she first attracted the notice of the King. A few years afterward she was created a duchess and, as such, retained the royal favor for a time. Then remorse seized upon La Vallière; she took the veil, and, as Sister Louise of Mercy, entered a convent, and gave her life in religious solitude to expiate the grief that she had caused the good Queen. The atonement was only just, for Louise de Vallière had made Marie Thérèse suffer bitterly the tortures of jealousy and offended conjugal affection. The Queen was not a woman of unusual intelligence, but she was sensible, tactful, and had a certain native dignity that compelled respect. She was, moreover, devoutly religious and devotedly attached to her children. She shared her royal Husband's conviction as to the divine right of kings, and what he did she considered could not be wrong. Of all the women that were associated with Louis, no one more truly admired him nor was more ardently devoted to him than his Queen. When they were first married, Louis treated Marie Thérèse with kindly consideration. He shed tears of sympathy and anguish while she suffered in giving birth to her first child. During the following dozen years, Marie Thérèse bore six sons and daughters, but all were lost except the Dauphin, and he died before ascending the throne. These bereavements sank deep into her heart and left a wound there that never healed. Added to this was the spectacle that she was called on repeatedly to witness of the King's infidelities with a succession of favorites. She was compelled to take these women into her household and make companions of them, knowing the while that they were really her rivals and persecutors. She was often heard to cry out concerning one or other of the favorites, "That woman will be the death of me." La Vallière she could afford to forgive, for the first mistress paid for the brief royal favor that she enjoyed by thirty-six years of rigid and austere penitence. Other favorites, however, pursued a path of pride, lowering their heads only under the "bludgeonings of Fate." Yet most of them, while Marie Thérèse lived, respected and honored her and felt a certain sense of shame in her presence. The brilliant and beautiful Madame de Montespan said, some time before her scandalous relations with the King had fairly begun, "God preserve me from being the King's mistress. If I were so I should feel ashamed to face the Queen." And yet Madame de Montespan, within a short time, assumed the role of favorite, and carried it out with great pride and arrogant assurance. The conviction is forced upon us, however, by the evidence of those that witnessed her ascendancy, that Montespan frequently felt the stings of self-reproach when she met the Queen, and that her haughty bearing concealed a genuine sense of shame. In the midst of luxury, power and brilliant success she seemed at times a small and mean character in the presence of the pious Marie Thérèse. As Louis' infidelities increased in number, his sense of guilt toward his consort was stamped deeper on his consciousness. He endeavored to make amends by paying her marked respect and treating her at times with distinguished tenderness and consideration. But Versailles was the high seat of elaborate and elegant insincerity, and no one was deceived by the formal courtesies paid by the Sun King to his unhappy wife. The deference that he displayed toward her in public appeared to the eyes of the world to be simply a cloak for essential neglect. And she, poor creature, with all the prestige of the Queen of France, was but a pitiful thing in the presence of the King. She tried to do her best to please him. The thought of offense to the Monarch beset her with fear. The Princess Palatine wrote of her once: "When the King came to her she was so gay that people remarked it. She would laugh and twinkle and rub her little hands. She had such a love for the King that she tried to catch in his eyes every hint of the things that would give him pleasure. If he ever looked at her kindly, that day was bright." Madame De Caylus tells us that the Queen had such a dread of her royal husband and such an inborn timidity that she hardly dared speak to him. Madame de Maintenon relates that the King, having once sent for the Queen, asked Madame to accompany Her Majesty so that she might not have to appear alone in the presence of her royal husband, and that when Madame de Maintenon conducted the Queen to the door of the King's room, and there took the liberty of pushing her ahead so as to force her to enter, she observed that Marie Therese fell into such a great tremble that her very hands shook with fright. And why should not the Queen tremble with unhappy apprehension when even the greatest favorite of all, Madame de Maintenon, found nothing in the life of the Court but bitter striving and heart misery? In the very midst of her splendor she exclaimed to a friend, "If I could only make clear to you the hideous _ennui_ that devours all of us, the troubles that fill our days! Do you not see that I am dying of sadness in the midst of a fortune that passes all imagination? I have had youth and beauty, I have sated myself with pleasure, I have had my hours of intellectual satisfaction, I have enjoyed royal favor, and yet I protest to you, my good friend, that all these conditions leave only a dreadful void."

Marie Thérèse took up her abode at Versailles only when the palace was pronounced complete. She entered her apartments there in 1682, and breathed her last in July of the following year. The Queen's bedroom is filled with historic memories. The walls could whisper many tragic secrets and the halls might assemble by invocation innumerable ghostly figures of fair women that once stood close to the throne, wore royal robes, and nursed breaking hearts. In the Queen's bed chamber died Marie Therese and, later, Marie Leczinska, the Queen of Louis XV. There also the Dauphiness of Bavaria and the Duchess of Burgundy passed away; and, in that chamber, nineteen princes and princesses of the royal blood were born, among whom were King Philip V of Spain and Louis XV of France. The chamber was occupied first by the pious and devoted Marie Therese; after that by the Bavarian Dauphiness, who died in 1690 at the early age of twenty-nine; then by the Duchess of Burgundy, the mother of Louis XV. She died in 1712 at the age of twenty-six. Then Mary Anne Victoire, the Infanta of Spain, occupied the apartment for a brief time; after that, in 1725, came Marie Leczinska, the wife of Louis XV, who lived there for forty-three years, during which she gave birth to ten children. And, finally, the most appealing figure of all entered that fateful apartment--she who has been characterized as "the most poetic of women, who combined in herself all majesties and all sorrows, all triumphs and all humiliations, all feminine joys and tears, she whose very name inspires the emotion, tenderness and respect of the world"--Marie Antoinette.

During the hundred years that followed the entrance of Marie Thérèse on the scene at Versailles, many extraordinary women came, shone and passed away. The Hall of Mirrors, had it the power to reflect the past, would afford a gallery of brilliant portraits. There would be, first, the devout Queen herself, virtuous, kind, considerate, loved by all her people and gently resigned to her fate. Then would follow a glittering train of proud and brilliant mistresses, some compelling by their beauty and gayety, others by their wit and sense. Sweet Madame de La Vallière had scarcely passed into obscurity when the haughty and imperious Marquise de Montespan assumed supremacy and became "the center of pleasures, of fortune, of hope and of terror to all that were dependent on the Court." No one could rightly claim to be an intimate of Montespan except the King, and at times he did not understand her. While apparently frank and free in her enjoyment of life and in her dealings with associates in the Court, Montespan always withheld enough to keep her best friends guessing. No one knew all her romance. She had experienced both extremes of fortune and when she gained favor with Louis she had acquired a confidence and a command of herself that influenced the King to a degree that even he would not have acknowledged. But the Court knew well the influence of Montespan and also the ministers, generals of the army and foreign ambassadors. Montespan succeeded Madame de La Vallière in favor about 1667 and she held her supremacy for ten years. Then came the turn of her fortunes, for Madame de Maintenon, fascinating in all that makes feminine charm and with an extraordinary mind in addition, supplanted Montespan and became the companion of the King until his dying day. Montespan, who had eight children by the King, left the Court in bitterness and humiliation and, like La Vallière, ended her life in a convent.

Madame de Maintenon was the most distinguished woman in the history of Versailles. As a girl, in abject poverty, she married in 1652 the good old poet Scarron. There was no love lost there. She merely took the gentle-hearted man because he offered either to pay for her entrance into a convent or to make her his wife, and she found the latter alternative more acceptable. During the nine years she lived with Scarron, she maintained a brilliant salon, in which gathered the great intellectual figures of the time. In 1669 Madame de Montespan gave Madame de Maintenon the charge of one of her sons. In that manner Montespan brought her governess in touch with her King, and, in so doing, sealed her own fate.

Madame de Maintenon was a very wise woman. She did not entertain any sincere affection for the King, and, during all the years of his devotion to her, she never really loved him. She found a monarch much sated with the luxurious pleasures of the Court, and beginning to tire of his latest mistress, and she saw in the situation an opportunity that appealed to her ambition. With shrewd judgment she measured the character of Madame de Montespan, and she forecast in her mind the inevitable downfall of the proud and arrogant favorite. She was the very opposite in nature of Madame de Montespan. Her self-possession, poise, skill and tact, virtue and piety made an irresistible appeal to the tired King. That her piety was scarcely more than a cloak is betrayed by many of her own utterances. "Nothing is more clever than irreproachable behavior," she said at one time to close friends. Her behavior was both irreproachable and clever, and it obtained for her the satisfaction of her highest ambitions. She fascinated and lured the King, playing the coquette to him, but evading him with a baffling assumption of virtue, yielding just enough to draw the Monarch on; then playing the part of a prude, until, finally, she became in the eyes of the fascinated Louis the most desired of women. It was not long before Madame de Maintenon was so advanced in the King's favor that the affair was the gossip of the Court, and Madame de Montespan was compelled to stand by, a silent and bitter witness of her own defeat. It was a humiliating blow to Madame de Montespan to see the King with eyes only for Madame de Maintenon, saying witty and agreeable things to her, and ignoring his former favorite completely. It was not long before Madame de Montespan received her dismissal and, trembling with rage, descended the great staircase of Versailles never again to mount it. Madame de Maintenon was installed in special apartments at the head of the Marble Staircase, opposite the Hall of the King's Guards, and a new spirit dominated the halls of the palace. Under Madame de Montespan a "haughtiness in everything that reached to the clouds" had held the Court and attendants in fear, made the lives of all uneasy, and kept the atmosphere of the palace astir. With the entrance of Madame de Maintenon into favor a quieter tone pervaded Versailles. Madame was a woman of great intelligence and wit, and made all feel the gracious influence of her fine companionship. There was nothing ascetic in her piety, but, on the other hand, frivolity, immorality, and unworthy intrigue had no place in her circle. And all those that attended her held her in esteem and profound respect. With all her incomparable grace, she was in mind and spirit more truly the queen than mistress. She was older than the King and her influence was stronger on that account. She had comprehended the situation at Versailles with characteristic shrewdness. The King needed her. The Court of France needed her--and she needed both the King and the Court for the fulfillment of her supreme ambitions. As one writer has ironically put it, "With her gracious bearing and her calm, even temper, she must have seemed to a king of forty-six, who had buried his queen and cast off his mistress, the ideal wife for his old age. Then, too, she was pious and devout, she wished to withdraw the King from the world and give him to God; she had no ambitions (!), she desired to meddle in nothing, she was grateful when her husband took her into his confidence, but she longed only to save his soul. It seemed almost too wonderful to be true. It was not true."

Madame de Maintenon was determined to be Queen of France, and she became so in soul as well as in fact. During her latter years she ruled, and the King was content to follow her advice and do her will. When the King was dying and she could gain no more at his hands, Madame de Maintenon effected a most satisfactory settlement for herself at St. Cyr, where she ended her days in piety and serene repose.

Saint-Amand has observed truly that the women of Versailles were interesting not only from the moral point of view and as subjects of study, but on account of what he called the "symbolical importance of their relations to the history of France." Each seemed to be the living expression of the spirit of her day. Madame de Montespan was just such a superb, luxurious and magnificent beauty as Versailles needed to display to all the ambassadors that came to bask in the glitter of the Sun King's Court. She was the dazzling mistress that ruled imperiously over the gay and brilliant life of the palace, the very incarnation of haughty and triumphant France at the culminating point of the reign of Louis XIV.

Then came Madame de Maintenon who, with her discreet and temperate nature, restored order, and was, for years, the living symbol of a changed condition in the Court in which piety and religious observance displaced licentious and voluptuous pleasure. And, along with this "wisdom of a repentant age," as Saint-Amand observes, "this reaction of austerity against pleasure, there was still the contrast of youth." It was the Duchess of Burgundy who was the living embodiment of this protest of joy against sadness, of springtime against cold winter, of licentiousness against the exacting restrictions of etiquette. Affairs in the Court had reached a turning point, and it was the logical mind of Madame de Maintenon that saw it. When Madame de Montespan was in the ascendancy, the Court had reached a condition of voluptuous indulgence that could not continue long. The Princess Palatine, wife of the brother of Louis XIV, wrote: "I hear and see every day so many villainous things that it disgusts me with life. You have good reason to say that the good Queen is now happier than we are, and if any one would do me, as to her and her mother, the service of sending me in twenty-four hours from this world to the other, I would certainly bear him no ill will."

However we may question the soul sincerity of Madame de Maintenon, to her at least we must give credit for checking the corrupt tendencies of the Court and, with correcting finger, pointing the way toward better things. After Louis XIV, as Saint-Amand points out, the conditions of the Court of France were reflected even more vividly in the characters of the women of Versailles. "With compression and reserve," he observes, "there followed scandal. During the regency and the reign of Louis XV the morals of the Court fast deteriorated. A new epoch opened--troublous, lewd, dissolute. And was not the Duchess of Berry eccentric, capricious, passionate, the very image of the time? The favorites of Louis XV indicate to us in their own sad history the conditions of debasing humiliation and moral decadence of monarchical power. At first Louis XV chose his favorites from among ladies of quality--after that, from the middle classes, and, finally, from the common women of the people." He did not stop at the low-born shop girl or the frequenter of evil resorts.

Louis began with the Duchesse de Châteauroux, the exquisite, who lasted, as we might say, but a day. From that he turned to the Marquise de Pompadour, a descent sufficiently significant, but it was only the beginning of decadence. The King's feeling for the Marquise was wholly unworthy, and it soon wore itself out. Her death caused him no regret. On the day of her funeral, during a heavy rainstorm, the King, standing at one of the windows of Versailles, watched the carriage bearing the body of his former favorite to Paris, and observed carelessly: "The Marquise will not have fine weather for her journey." Louis soon turned to Madame Dubarry--and a lower step was taken. The prestige and dignity of the Court suffered. "Vice," as Saint-Amand observes, "threw off all semblance of disguise" and yet, while the King slowly submerged his nature in a slough of corruption, and his associates made of the Court a carnival of immorality, there was still one figure in whom the traditional morals and manners were maintained-- the Queen Marie Leczinska. She was the one pure and virtuous figure in the Court life. "Her domestic hearth," writes Saint-Amand, "was near the boudoir of the favorites, but it was she that preserved for the Court the traditions of decency and decorum.

"Last of all of the women of Versailles, came Marie Antoinette, the woman who, in the most striking and tragic of all destinies, represents not solely the majesty and the griefs of royalty, but all the graces and all the agonies, all the joys and all the sufferings, of her sex."

CHAPTER VIII
THE VERSAILLES OF LOUIS XV

Louis the Great, in commanding immense and costly edifices to rise out of the earth, was moved, at least in part, by a desire to assure the monarchy and its established ceremonial a worthy background. Louis XV, in the numerous graceful additions to the chateau made by him, sought only to satisfy his own caprice and convenience.

When the Court returned from Vincennes to Versailles in 1722, seven years after the death of Louis XIV, one of the new King's first undertakings was the construction of the Salon of Hercules, adjoining the chapel court. This splendid hall, which to-day serves as the entrance to the _grand appartements_, owed its design to Robert de Cotte. As in the time of Louis XIV and Mansard, marble was chosen as the main decorative medium. All the sculptural ornaments are in bronze and marble. The bases of the pilasters are of gilded bronze. Carvings in wood and stucco were contributed by a Flemish artist named Verberckt, to whom Louis XV assigned most of the sculptural work done at the chateau during his reign. It was he that modeled the two doors placed on either side the bronze and marble chimney-piece, and the sculptures of the cornice. The painting on the ceiling--the Apotheosis of Hercules--was first seen by His Majesty as he passed through the room on his way to mass on a day in September, 1736. He examined it with much attention (some one has taken the trouble to record), and demonstrated his satisfaction by forthwith naming Sire Le Moine, the creator of the work, his chief painter. And thereon hangs a tragic tale. So great was Le Moine's pride in the honor thus done him that he determined to bring his work to still higher perfection. He resolved to finish each detail with the same exactitude as though he were painting a canvas that was to be observed at close range. But the more he applied his brush to bring out intricate effects, the less the design pleased him. In a sudden revulsion for the completed work, he effaced it and began the entire painting anew. This time he was better satisfied, though critics attached to the Court esteemed the second canvas not so good as the one destroyed. Upon the completion of the decorative scheme, the Sovereign bestowed upon Le Moine 5,000 _livres_ for the _Salon d'Hercule_. Then, to his chagrin, the over-careful artist discovered that he was out of pocket 24,000 _livres_ by the transaction. The loss turned his head; seized by grief and disappointment he committed suicide.

This salon served during the reign of Louis XV as a ball-room, and here in March, 1749, the Monarch was formally presented with two young ostriches, brought from Egypt and destined for the Menagerie.

In contrast to the passion for ostentation exhibited by Louis XIV, his great-grandson and successor was chiefly occupied in finding ways to evade his gilded prison. When the demand of the Court necessitated his presence at Versailles, he sought diversion in changing the apartments, making them over, demolishing here, reconstructing there--expending vast sums at all times. In 1738, finding the chamber of Louis XIV cold and inconvenient, he ordered another suite to be arranged for him on the second floor of the chateau above the Marble Court, and here he lived at his ease, untrammeled by etiquette and far from the curious gaze of courtiers. Small living rooms, kitchens, grills and bakeries were built on the Court of the Stags, and above the private apartments of Louis XIV rooms were added for the favorites of the King.

The storied Staircase of the Ambassadors, by which ceremonious visitors were admitted to the presence of the Sun King, was leveled by the whim of Louis XV. Little mattered it to him that this superb entrance filled an essential role in the life of the royal residence. Forgetful of the scenes that had been enacted on the triumphal stair, the great-grandson of the builder of Versailles commanded the destruction of one of the noblest architectural works of the time. Its bas-reliefs, its incomparable marbles, its paintings on which Lebrun had exercised all the resources of his decorative genius--all disappeared at the nod of the ambitious Madame de Pompadour, who desired a theater to be erected on this site. In later years the theater disappeared to make room for the apartments of the King's fair daughter, Madame Adelaïde.

The project to build another flight of steps ending in the Salon of Hercules was never carried out. Future guests were therefore admitted to the reception rooms by a dark, narrow entrance, or they made a long roundabout tour by way of the Queen's staircase across the Marble Court. The demolition of the stairway of honor was an irreparable loss. No other piece of wantonness equaled it in the tumultuous history of Versailles.

However, there remain in the château a number of memorials to the judgment and good taste of the third master of the chateau, among them, the exquisitely decorated rooms of the King, re-made on the site of those dedicated to Louis XIV; the seven rooms of Madame Adelaide, and the suites set apart for the mistresses that succeeded one another in the favor of Louis the Fifteenth. These apartments, evolved out of the confusion of orders and counter-orders, remain to-day as examples of the pure and elegant decorative styles of the eighteenth century. Especially admired is the

Council Room. Richly adorned, but always in charming taste, it represents the transition period between the more severe ornamental art peculiar to the reign of Louis XIV and the warmer effects beloved by Louis XV. Behind the Council Room were installed, on the west side of the Court of the Stags, a _cabinet de bains_ (bath-room) and a little room called the Salon of the Wigs. By these rooms access was gained to the Salon of Apollo.

The billiard-room, where King Louis XIV was wont to play with his hounds before retiring, became the bed-room of his heir. After the year 1738, Louis XV occupied this chamber, and here he died thirty-six years later. It then became the sleeping-room of the ill-starred Louis XVI--who died in no bed. Locks, door-knobs, chimney ornaments--each detail in gilded bronze reflected rare taste and workmanship. The bed stood in an alcove enclosed between two columns, railed in by a balustrade of elaborate design, and curtained by wonderful tapestries. Ordinarily the King slept in this room; when he wakened in the morning he put on a robe and passed through the Council Room to the salon where the "rising" was celebrated with traditional pomp.

If Louis XV indulged in an orgy of building and repair, it was because he pined with an _ennui_ that was only relieved by constant diversion. If at the cost of unnumbered thousands of francs, Madame de Pompadour urged on her royal lover and contrived new outlets for his craze for building, it was because she was adroit enough to enliven by this means an existence that often palled upon him. If, throughout the long series of decisions and contradictions regarding changes in the chateau, the Monarch commanded one day that a library and marble bath be added to the apartments of his daughter, and on another that useful halls, staircases and offices be removed; if he ordered the construction of a great Opera House with a facade like a temple, and, in another mood, made away with insignificant rooms that consumed no more space than would have filled a remote corner of this great hall of the theater--the motive was ever the same: to banish for the time-being the hovering specter of boredom and melancholy. "Louis XV," comments the author of "France Under Louis XV," "was not a man that sought relief from ceremony and adulation in any useful work; but, on the other hand, this dull grandeur was not dear to his heart; he did not derive from it the majestic satisfaction that it furnished to his predecessor. From youth to age the King was bored; he wearied of his throne, his court, himself; he was indifferent to all things, and unconcerned as to the weal or the woe of his people."

One of the Salons on which he lavished all the art of his epoch was the reception-room of the royal Adelaïde. Here all was carved and gilded in a manner exquisite beyond words--chimney, doors, ceiling, window embrasures, mirror frames. Musical instruments were employed as sculpture _motifs_, for in this room the princess liked to sit and play her violoncello. In the dining-room, the decorative designs were delicately carved rosettes, arabesques, garlands of fruits and flowers, crowns and medallions.

The supreme ruler of Louis XV's affections--the amazing Madame Dubarry--was lodged "in a suite of delectable boudoirs" facing the Marble Court, above the private apartments of the King. Everywhere appeared the initial _L_ linked with the torches of Love. One of the objects most admired in the drawing-room was an English piano-forte, with a case adorned with rosewood medallions, blue and white mosaics and gilded metal. In this room there were chests of drawers of antique lacquer and ebony, statues of marble, and garnishings of sculptured bronze. At night all was ablaze with the lights of the great luster of rock-crystal that hung from the center of the ceiling, and had cost, it was said, a sum equaling three thousand American dollars. In varying form, but with equal richness, all the apartments of Dubarry were beautified at the King's behest.

In January, 1747, the "theater of the little apartments" of the King was inaugurated by a representation of "_Tartuffe_" with Madame de Pompadour in the cast. The King frequently permitted himself to be distracted with music and the play in this hall in the Little Gallery. Here was an orchestra of twenty-eight musicians, a ballet, and a chorus of twenty-six, under the direction of Monsieur de Bury, Lully's successor as master of the Court music. Actors, singers, dancers, all were supplied with gorgeous costumes, and given the services of Sire Notrelle, the most celebrated wig-maker in Paris, who had in his day a prodigious vogue. One of his advertisements announced his ability to imitate the coiffures of "gods, demons, heroes and shepherds, tritons, cyclops, naiads and furies." Astounding were the head-dresses of the actors and actresses that graced the stage of Versailles.

Invitations to a dramatic performance were given by the King himself, and, for many years, to men guests only. Sometimes the Pompadour played the comedies of Voltaire, whom she favored against the will of all the royal family. Occasionally, performances were of necessity postponed out of respect to a member of the Court that had been slain in a duel; but not for long did the King and his train pause in their restless pursuit of pleasure.

A new theater was installed, with more room for auditors, troupe and musicians. Finally, in 1753, the Opera House was begun according to designs submitted by Gabriel, first architect to the King. After long delays the edifice was completed in time for the marriage fêtes of the Dauphin (Louis XVI) and Marie Antoinette, Archduchess of Austria. The hall of the

Opera was so surpassingly fine in its dress of fine woodwork, green marble and gilding that a writer of the period, addressing a friend in Paris, where all were discontented with the Opera House just built in the capital, bade him "come with the crowd of curious folk to Versailles and admire the magnificent building of the Court Opera. Besides the beautiful outer view it presents," said he, "and the splendor of its ensemble, the mechanism of the interior is amazing." In this imposing auditorium the Court of Louis XVI heard the operas of Lully and Rameau, the tragedies of Racine and Voltaire. Here at a banquet in October, 1789, Louis XVI called on his supporters at Versailles to oppose the Revolution. And a short time later, the hall of the Opera served as a meeting-place for the insurrectionists.

In 1837, Louis Phillipe, last of the Bourbon kings, restored the building and redecorated it in red marble. In memory of Louis XIV, the reigning King commanded his troupe to perform a comedy by Molière. Extracts from Meyerbeer's opera, _Robert le Diable_, and a piece written by Auber concluded the fête organized by this monarch to recall the golden days of Louis the Superb.

When, in the summer of 1855, Napoleon III entertained Queen Victoria at Versailles, the supper that terminated a day of brilliant celebrations was laid in the banquet hall of the Opera. The last theatrical performance given in this worthy memorial to the building enterprise of Louis XV was witnessed by Napoleon III, Empress Eugénie, and the King of Spain.

CHAPTER IX
THE TWILIGHT OF THE BOURBON KINGS

It was on a May morning in the year 1770 that the child-bride of the Dauphin of France arrived at Versailles--the graceful, winsome, golden-haired Marie Antoinette, daughter of Maria Theresa, Empress of Austria. The future Queen of France was then not fifteen years of age, and her affianced husband was but a few months older.

A letter in her own hand, dated at Versailles on the 24th of May, 1770, describes the incidents of her ceremonious journey from Austria, and her reception by Louis XV and his heir. Other letters to her family give us glimpses of the wedding in the chapel of Versailles, of the fêtes, the balls at the palace, the function of distributing bread and wine to the people, the hunts in nearby forests, the dances, musicales and informal assemblages of the royal family in the intimate apartments of the chateau.

"Our life here is perpetual movement," wrote the Dauphine to her sister; and to her mother she sent this quaint epistle a few weeks after her arrival in France: "You wish to know how I spend my time habitually. I will say, therefore, that I rise at ten o'clock or nine, or half-past nine, and after dressing I say my prayers; then I breakfast, after which I go to my aunts' (Madame Adelaïde, Victoire and Sophie), where I usually meet the King. At eleven I go to have my hair dressed. At noon the Chambre is called, and any one of sufficient rank may come in. I put on my rouge and wash my hands before everybody; then the gentlemen go out; the ladies stay, and I dress before them. At twelve is mass; when the King is at Versailles I go to mass with him and my husband and my aunts. After mass we dine together before everybody, but it is over by half-past one, as we both eat quickly. (Marie Antoinette always found the custom of eating in public most distasteful.) I then go to Monsieur the Dauphin; if he is busy I return to my own apartments, where I read, I write, or I work, for I am embroidering a vest for the King, which does not get on quickly, but I trust that, with God's help, it will be finished in a few years! At three I go to my aunts', where the King usually comes at that time. At four the Abbé (her literary mentor) comes to me; at five the master for the harpsichord, or the singing-master, till six. At half-past six I generally go to my aunts' when I do not go out. You must know that my husband almost always comes with me to my aunts'. At seven, card-playing till nine. When the weather is fine I go out; then the card-playing takes place in my aunts' apartments instead of mine. At nine, supper; when the King is absent my aunts come to take supper with us; if the King is there, we go to them after supper, and we wait for the King, who comes usually at a quarter before eleven; but I lie on a large sofa and sleep till his arrival; when he is not expected we go to bed at eleven. Such is my day.

"I entreat you, my very dear mother, to, forgive me if my letter is too long. I ask pardon also for the blotted letter, but I have had to write two days running at my toilet, having no other time at my disposal."

In the winter the Court made merry with sleighing, skating and dancing parties, and formal affairs in honor of foreign princes. "There is too much etiquette here to live the family life," lamented the child to her mother. "Altogether, the Court at Versailles is a little dull, the formalities are so fatiguing. But I am happy, for Monsieur the Dauphin is very polite to me and always attentive." In another letter she recounted the triumph attending the first presentation of the opera _Iphigénie_, by Gluck. "The Dauphin applauded everything and Gluck showed himself very well pleased. . . . He has written me some pieces that I sing to the harpsichord."

Several times a week, the awkward, bashful boy who was to become Louis XVI of France pleased his light-hearted wife by taking dancing lessons with her. Hours were spent with him in the park at Versailles, skipping about, laughing, playing pranks like the little girl she was. Sometimes there were charades, and plays by amateurs and professionals behind the "closed doors" of their own rooms.

In 1774, four years after the marriage of Marie Antoinette to the Dauphin, Louis XV was taken ill of smallpox during a sojourn at the Little Trianon, and was removed to Versailles. Within a fortnight he was dead, and a scandalous reign was ended. "The rush of the courtiers, with a noise like thunder, as they hastened to pay homage to the new sovereign," says a narrator of the Queen's story, "was the first announcement of the great event to the young heir and his wife." The new King had not yet reached his twentieth year. "God help and protect us!" they both cried on their knees. "We are too young to reign!"

As Queen of France, Marie Antoinette occupied a series of superbly appointed rooms in the left wing of the palace. Beyond a dark passageway were her husband's apartments. Her bed-chamber was the scene of the formal toilet, a ceremony always irksome to the youthful sovereign. In this sumptuous room, where queens had borne kings-to-be, and had closed their eyes forever upon a melancholy existence, she gave birth to four children. The royal bed was raised on steps and surrounded by a gilt balustrade; nearby was a gorgeously fitted dressing-table. There were also armchairs, we are told, with down cushions, "tables for writing, and two chests of drawers of elaborate workmanship. The curtains and hangings were of rich but plain blue silk. The stools for those that had the privilege of being seated in the royal presence, with a sofa for the Queen's use, were placed against the walls, according to the formal custom of the time. The canopy of the bed was adorned with Cupids playing with garlands and holding gilt lilies, the royal flower."

Other rooms prepared for the Queen faced an inner court, and here with music, small talk and embroidery she spent contented moments, remote from the demands of her high estate.

Usually the mistress of Versailles was wakened at eight o'clock by a lady of the bedchamber, whose first duty it was to proffer a ponderous volume containing samples of the dresses that were in the royal wardrobe. Marie Antoinette marked with pins, taken from an embroidered cushion, the costumes she wished to put on for the various events of the day--the brocaded and hooped Court dress for the morning mass, the negligee to be worn during leisure hours in her own living rooms, and the gown to be donned for evening festivities. These vital matters determined, the Queen proceeded with her bath and her breakfast of chocolate and rolls. She was accustomed then to return to bed, and, with her tapestry-work in hand, receive various persons attached to her service. Physicians, reader, secretary, came to ask her wishes and do her bidding. At noon followed the "rising," and the stately progress of the Queen and her attendants through the Salon of Peace to the dazzling Hall of Mirrors, where the King awaited her on his way to chapel. Often at this hour there were admitted to the Grand Gallery of Mirrors respectful groups of commoners, who gathered to watch the passing of the gracious Marie Antoinette beside the husband whose uncouth gait and features were ever in forbidding contrast to her own comely bearing.

Amid all the follies and splendors of life at Versailles appeared the sturdy American figure of Dr. Benjamin Franklin. In the year 1767 he was presented at Court on the occasion of his first visit to Paris.

"You see," said he, in a letter to Miss Stevenson, daughter of his landlady in London, "I speak of the Queen as if I had seen her; and so I have, for you must know I have been at Court. We went to Versailles last Sunday, and had the honor of being presented to the King, Louis XV. In the evening we were at the _Grand Convert_, where the family sup in public. The table was half a hollow square, the service of gold. . . . An officer of the Court brought us up through the crowd of spectators, and placed Sir John (Pringle) so as to stand between the Queen and Madame Victoire. The King talked a good deal to Sir John, and did me, too, the honor of taking some notice of me.

"Versailles has had infinite sums laid out in building it and supplying it with water. Some say the expenses exceeded eighty millions sterling

($400,000,000). The range of buildings is immense; the garden-front most magnificent, all of hewn stone; the number of statues, figures, urns, etc., in marble and bronze of exquisite workmanship, is beyond conception. But the water-works are out of repair, and so is a great part of the front next the town, looking, with its shabby, half-brick walls, and broken windows, not much better than the houses in Durham Yard. There is, in short, both at Versailles and Paris, a prodigious mixture of magnificence and negligence with every kind of elegance except that of cleanliness, and what we call tidiness."

Franklin next appeared at the Court of Versailles upon the momentous occasion of the ratification of the alliance signed in 1778 by France and America. Dressed in a black velvet suit with ruffles of snowy white, white silk stockings and silver buckles, the emissary of the United States appeared in a gorgeous coach at the portals of Versailles. It is related that the chamberlain hesitated a moment to admit him, for he was without the wig and sword Court etiquette demanded, "but it was only for a moment; and all the Court were captivated at the democratic effrontery of his conduct." Franklin and the four envoys that accompanied him were conducted to the dressing-room of Louis XVI, who, without ceremony, assured them of his friendship for the new-born country they represented. In the evening the Americans were invited to watch the play of the royal family at the gaming-table, and Dr. Franklin, so Madame Campan relates, "was honored by the particular notice of the Queen, who courteously desired him to stand near to her, and as often as the game did not require her immediate attention, she took occasion to speak to him in very obliging terms."

The _New York Journal_, under date of July 6, 1778, recounted another picturesque detail of this presentation of the American envoys at Versailles. When they entered the inner part of the palace, so the dispatch ran, "they were received by _les Cents Suisses_ (Swiss Guards), the major of which announced, '_Les Ambassadeurs des treize provinces unies_,' i.e., The Ambassadors from the Thirteen United Provinces."

During the Revolution in America the newspapers made much of Marie Antoinette's liking for Benjamin Franklin. Among others, the _New Hampshire Gazette_ printed this story, which went the rounds of the States. "Franklin being lately in the gardens of Versailles, showing the Queen some electrical experiment, she asked him in a fit of raillery if he did not dread the fate of Prometheus, who was so severely served for stealing fire from Heaven. 'Yes, please your Majesty' (replied old Franklin, with infinite gallantry), 'if I did not behold a pair of eyes pass unpunished which have stolen infinitely more fire from Jove than I ever did, though they do more mischief in a week than I have done in all my experiments.'"

On January 20, 1783, at the office of the Count de Vergennes at Versailles, in the presence of Dr. Franklin and Mr. Adams, the representatives of England, France and Spain affixed their signatures to the preliminary documents declaring war at an end between America and England. A little over seven months later, on September 3, 1783, at the Hotel de York in Paris, the final treaty between Great Britain and the United States was signed. Later on the same day, the definitive treaty between England and France was concluded at Versailles. When Franklin was about to take leave of France and return to Philadelphia, Louis XVI presented to him the royal portrait, framed by 408 diamonds, the value of which was estimated at $10,000.

No less than his predecessor had the new Monarch of Versailles and his gay, ease-loving, oft-times imprudent young wife disregarded the traditions and dignity of the Sun King's palace. If Louis XV demolished the Staircase of the Ambassadors and mutilated the _grands appartements_, Marie Antoinette imitated his desecrations in the royal dwelling by commanding any change that pleased her fancy, by reducing rooms of state to mere private chambers, and shutting herself off from the irritating claims of Court life. Many of the trees in the park died that had been set out at the proud command of Louis XIV. The gardens became neglected and desolate. The famous Labyrinth of Aesop's fountains disappeared.

A grove planted on the place formerly beautified by the Grotto of Thetis (or Tethys) gave sanctuary to the impious scheming of that Madame de Lamotte, whose intrigue and evil ambition brought upon the Queen in 1785 the scandal of the Diamond Necklace, with the subsequent dramatic arrest of Cardinal de Rohan in the fateful Hall of Mirrors, and the humiliating trial of Marie Antoinette.

Bored by incessant publicity, finding no pleasure in the formal promenades of the palace park, the Queen pleaded for "a house of her own," where she could find recreation after her own tastes, unobserved by the curious and the critical. Louis XV had built near the Grand Trianon a small villa for Madame de Pompadour. On the modest estate were several small outbuildings, to which were added a pavilion for open-air pastimes and a "French garden." It was Gabriel, architect of the Opera House, that drew the plans for the little chateau, begun in 1762. But Madame de Pompadour died before the villa of her fancy was completed. Dubarry succeeded her as chatelaine, and richly embellished the interior of the delectable retreat.

When Marie Antoinette desired to possess a _maison de plaisance_ of which she should be sole mistress, the King, always eager to satisfy her whims, bade her accept for her own use both the Grand and the Petit Trianon. Said he, graciously, "These charming houses have always been the repair of favorites of the reigning king--consequently they should now be yours." The Queen was much pleased with the gift and with her husband's gallantry. She responded, laughingly, that she would accept the Little Trianon on condition that he would not come there except when invited!

During the tenancy of Marie Antoinette, some of the rooms of the Petit Trianon were altered according to the elaborate style that received the name of Louis XVI. Sculptures, wood-work, gilded chimneys, staircases, were fashioned by the hands of master artists. No sooner was she possessor of her new domain than the Queen desired a garden after the pastoral English style that was then coming in favor. A lake, a stream with ornamental bridges, clusters of trees, supplanted the symmetrical design of a botanical garden that had been much admired. A gallant attached to the Court wrote an _Elégie_ in praise of the Petit Trianon, its flowers, tulip trees and fragrant walks. At one end of the lake a hamlet was created, with a picture-mill and a dairy, fitted with marble tables and cream jugs of rare porcelain. There was also a farm where the Queen pastured a splendid herd of Swiss cattle. Among these bucolic surroundings the King of France, forgetful of his people and their growing anguish, played shepherd to his shepherdess Queen. In the Temple of Love they basked on summer days among rosy vines, while the music of Court players wafted through the trees from a nearby pavilion. Every Sunday during the summer season there was a ball in the park, where any one might dance whose clothes and behavior were respectable. The Queen, sensing the need to propitiate a disgruntled populace, shared in the afternoon's revelries, petted the children that flocked about her knees, chatted with their nurses and parents. Often, Marie Antoinette resided for weeks at a time at her favorite dwelling, fishing in the lake, tending her herd, picking berries in her garden patch. The King and the princes came every day for supper, and were received by a Queen dressed in white with a fichu of net--sometimes in a "rumpled gown of cotton." A score of favorites composed the Court of the Little Trianon. All others were excluded. Heavy silks and towering head-dresses were forgotten in the simple life of the Petit Trianon. Tiresome etiquette was banished, together with thoughts of international matters of portent and impending calamity. Occasionally, comedies were given, or groves and canal were illuminated in honor of a visitor of high degree--the Emperor Joseph of Austria (brother of the Queen), the King of Sweden, ambassadors, princes, archduchesses.

Surrounded by the persons and the objects she most loved--free to go and come unattended by a train of attendants--those were the least unhappy days in the life of Marie Antoinette at Versailles.

At the Little Trianon, Madame Vigée Lebrun made, in 1787, the painting of Marie Antoinette with her children, which the Queen's intimates counted the truest likeness among all her portraits. Two years later, on the fifth day of October, the Queen was at Trianon when news came of the approach of the mob of starving, angry women that stormed the road from Paris, swept across the Place d'Armes, and surged about the doors of the despised palace. On that day, Marie Antoinette left her "little house," never to see it again.

For many months the clouds had been gathering on the horizon of the Bourbon King, whose extravagance and weak will were matched by the childish indiscretions of his Austrian consort.

In November, 1787, the Notables assembled at Versailles in the grand hall of the palace guards. In May, 1789, the Salon of Hercules witnessed the presentation of the twelve hundred deputies elected by the people in all parts of France to the States-General. The Assembly, "the true era of the birth of the French people," opened on May fifth in the immense _Salle des Menus_, on the Paris Avenue, outside the gates of the palace. During the thirty days that the deputies sat inactive under the oratory of the King, of Necker, Mirabeau and Robespierre, work ceased throughout the kingdom. "He who had but his hands, his daily labor, to supply the day, went to look for work, found none, begged, got nothing, robbed. Starving gangs overran the country; wherever they found any resistance, they became furious, killed, and burned. Horror spread far and near; communications ceased, and famine went on increasing." At last the Assembly was founded, but the nation remained in tumult, the King vacillating, the Queen in retirement, mourning the death of the little Dauphin. On June twentieth, the people's representatives gathered, in spite of the King, in the bare tennis-court, without the walls of the chateau, and made oath as citizens of France never to adjourn until they had given their country a constitution. On the same day Marie Antoinette inscribed a letter from Versailles whose import was in piteous contrast to the prattling epistles of her girlhood. "The Chambre Nationale is declared," she wrote. "They are deliberating, but I am in despair to see nothing come of their deliberations; every one is greatly alarmed. The nobility may be wiped out forever. But the kingdom will be calm; if not, one cannot estimate the evils by which we shall be menaced. . . . Not far away civil war exists, and, besides, bread is lacking. God give us courage!" Three days later the King read to the deputies an arbitrary declaration that had been composed by interested advisers. He commanded the assembly to disperse, and met a calm and silent resistance. Workmen entered to demolish the amphitheater, but laid down their tools on the declaration of Mirabeau that "whoever laid hands on a deputy was a traitor, infamous and worthy of death." At last the King, wearied and confused, commanded, "Let them alone."

The parterres, the courts, even the salons of the palace swarmed with ruffians that had marched out from Paris to menace Versailles. By June 25th there was open revolt in the capital. "A stormy, heavy, gloomy time, like a feverish, painful dream," prefaced the furious deeds of the 14th of July. Every day witnessed some new outbreak. July was a month of insurrections and murders. The Bastille was assailed by rioters. News came to the King that the ancient fortress had fallen. "Sire," announced the Duke of Orleans to the sleepy Monarch in his bedchamber, "it is a Revolution!"

Lafayette, back from the war across the sea, became the unwilling leader of the National Guard. On the evening of the first of October occurred the fatal banquet of the King's guard, held, not in the Orangery or in some other informal hall, but in the palace theater, where no fête had been given since the visit of the Emperor Joseph II of Austria. A French writer describes the scene. "The doors open. Behold the King and the Queen! The King has been prevailed on to visit them on his return from the chase. The Queen walks round to every table, looking beautiful, and adorned with the child she bears in her arms.

"So beautiful and yet so unfortunate! As she was departing with the King, the band played the affecting air: 'O Richard, O my King, abandoned by the whole world!' Every heart melted at that appeal. Several tore off their cockades, and took that of the Queen, the black Austrian cockade, devoting themselves to her service. . . .

"On the 3rd of October, another dinner; they grow more daring, their tongues are untied, and the counter-revolution showed itself boldly. In the long gallery, and in the apartments, the ladies no longer allow the tricolor cockade to circulate. With their handkerchiefs and ribands they make white cockades, and tie them themselves."

Stories of royalist revels and open insults to the cockade of the Revolutionists still further inflamed starving Paris. On the fifth of October there were thousands of inhabitants that had tasted no food for thirty hours. And then the ravenous women of Paris arose--mothers, shop-girls, courtesans--and, gathering recruits as they swept through the restless city streets, they rolled like an angry flood out the eleven-mile road to Versailles. The King was hunting at Meudon; a courier was sent for him. The Queen Consort was in her retreat at Trianon. The messenger found her, sad and contemplative, seated in her grotto. Hastily she was brought back to the palace. Later, she and the King would have fled the anger of the crowd whose shouts of "Bread! Bread!" echoed across the Marble Court to the windows of the royal apartments. But their decision, put off from moment to moment, came too late. The gates were closed. They were prisoners within the walls of Versailles.

"It was a rainy night," relates a French historian of the Revolution. "The crowd took shelter where they could; some burst open the gates of the great stables, where the regiment of Flanders was stationed, and mixed pell-mell with the soldiers. Others, about four thousand in number, had remained in the Assembly. The men were quiet enough, but the women were impatient at that state of inaction; they talked, shouted, and made an uproar.

"The King's heart was beginning to fail him; he perceived that the Queen was in peril. However agonizing it was to his conscience to consecrate the legislative work of philosophy, at ten o'clock in the evening he signed the Declaration of Rights.

"Mounier was at last able to depart. He hastened to resume his place as president before the arrival of that vast army from Paris, whose projects were not yet known. He reentered the hall; but there was no longer any Assembly; it had broken up; the crowd, ever growing more clamorous and exacting, had demanded that the prices of bread and meat should be lowered. Mounier found in his place, in the president's chair, a tall, fine, well-behaved woman, holding the bell in her hand, who left the chair with reluctance. He gave orders that they were to try to collect the deputies again; meanwhile, he announced to the people that the King had just accepted the constitutional article. The women, crowding about him, then entreated him to give them copies of them; others said: 'But, Monsieur President, will this be very advantageous? Will this give bread to the poor people of Paris?' Others exclaimed: 'We are very hungry. We have eaten nothing to-day.' Mounier ordered bread to be fetched from the bakers. Provisions then came in on all sides. They all began eating in the hall with much clamour."

At midnight Lafayette arrived at the head of twenty thousand men of the National Guard. To the amazement of the soldiers and onlookers, he dared to pass unattended through the palace doors to the Bull's Eye. "He appeared very calm," says Madame de Staël, Necker's observant daughter. "Nobody ever saw him otherwise." When he had reported his arrival to the King, Lafayette stationed guards about the palace, and, worn with hours of marching in the rain and mud, so far forgot his duty to his Sovereign and his command that he retired to his house in the town of Versailles to seek sleep. In the masses of people outside the gates were thieves and men of violence. "What a delightful prospect was opened for pillage in the wonderful palace of Versailles, where the riches of France had been amassed for more than a century!" exclaims the commentator, Michelet. Here follows a dramatic account of what followed, based on the story of Madame de Staël, who witnessed many of the bloody scenes in person. "At five in the morning, before daylight, a large crowd was already prowling about the gates, armed with pikes, spits, and scythes. About six o'clock, this crowd, composed of Parisians and people of Versailles, scale or force the gates, and advance into the courts with fear and hesitation. The first who was killed, if we believe the Royalists, died from a fall, having slipped in the Marble Court. According to another and a more likely version, he was shot dead by the body-guard.

"Some took to the left, toward the Queen's apartment, others to the right, toward the chapel stairs, nearer the King's apartment. On the left, a Parisian running unarmed, among the foremost, met one of the body guard, who stabbed him with a knife. The guardsman was killed. On the right, the foremost was a militia-man of the guard of Versailles, a diminutive locksmith, with sunken eyes, almost bald, and his hands chapped by the heat of the forge. This man and another, without answering the guard, who had come down a few steps and was speaking to him on the stairs, strove to pull him down by his belt, and hand him over to the crowd rushing behind. The guards pulled him towards them; but two of them were killed. They all fled along the Grand Gallery, as far as the _Oeil-de-boeuf_ (Bull's Eye), between the apartments of the King and the Queen. Other guards were already there.

"The most furious attack had been made in the direction of the Queen's apartment. The sister of her _femme de chambre_, Madame de Campan, having half opened the door, saw a guardsman covered with blood, trying to stop the furious rabble. She quickly bolted that door and the next, put a petticoat on the Queen, and tried to lead her to the King. An awful moment! The door was bolted on the other side! They knock again and again. The King was not within; he had gone round by another passage to reach the Queen. At that moment a pistol was fired, and then a gun close to them. 'My friends, my dear friends,' cried the Queen, bursting into tears, 'save me and my children!' At length the door was opened, and she rushed into the King's apartment.

"The crowd was knocking louder and louder to enter the _Oeil-de-boeuf_. The guards barricaded the place, piling up benches, stools, and other pieces of furniture; the lower panel was burst in. They expected nothing but death; but suddenly the uproar ceased, and a kind clear voice exclaimed: 'Open!' As they did not obey, the same voice repeated: 'Come, open to us, body-guard; we have not forgotten that you men saved us French Guards at Fontenoy.'

"It was indeed the French Guards, now become National Guards, with the brave and generous Hoche, then a simple sergeant-major--it was the people, who had come to save the nobility. They opened, threw themselves into one another's arms, and wept.

"At that moment, the King, believing the passage forced, and mistaking his saviors for his assassins, opened his door himself, by an impulse of courageous humanity, saying to those without: 'Do not hurt my guards.'

"The danger was past, and the crowd dispersed; the thieves alone were unwilling to be inactive. Wholly engaged in their own business, they were pillaging and moving away the furniture. The grenadiers turned that rabble out of the castle.

"Lafayette, awakened but too late, then arrived on horseback. He saw one of the body-guards whom they had taken and dragged near the body of one of those killed by the guards, in order to kill him by way of retaliation. 'I have given my word to the King,' cried Lafayette, 'to save his men. Cause my word to be respected.'

"He then entered the castle. Madame Adelaïde, the King's aunt, went up to him and embraced him: 'It is you,' cried she, 'who have saved us.' He ran to the King's cabinet. Who would believe that etiquette still subsisted? A grand officer stopped him for a moment, and then allowed him to pass: 'Sir,' said he seriously, 'the King grants you _les grandes entrées_.'

"The King showed himself at the balcony, and was welcomed with the unanimous shout of 'God save the King.' 'Vive le Roi!'

"At that moment several voices raised a formidable shout: 'The Queen!' The people wanted to see her in the balcony. She hesitated: 'What!' said she, 'all alone?' 'Madame, be not afraid,' said Lafayette. She went, but not alone, holding an admirable safeguard--in one hand her daughter, in the other her son. The Court of Marble was terrible, in awful commotion, like the sea in its fury; the National Guards, lining every side, could not answer for the center; there were fire-arms, and men blind with rage. Lafayette's conduct was admirable; for that trembling woman, he risked his popularity, his destiny, his very life; he appeared with her on the balcony, and kissed her hand.

"The crowd felt all that; the emotion was unanimous. They saw there the woman and the mother, nothing more. 'Oh! how beautiful she is! What! is that the Queen? How she fondles her children!'"

The King, overcome by dread, was forced to agree to the demand of the people that he go to Paris. In leaving his palace, he realized that he was finally surrendering all his claims to royalty. About noon on the sixth day of October, Louis XVI and Marie Antoinette, under the protection of the Marquis de Lafayette, turned their faces forever from Versailles. Little they knew that they were even then traveling the long road to the guillotine. A rabble of men and women surrounded them, some on foot, some in carts and carriages. "All were very merry and amiable in their own fashion, except a few jokes addressed to the Queen."

Such was the end of royal Versailles. Who can contest its tragic grandeur? In these halls, these gardens, these secluded villas the supreme destiny of the Bourbon monarchy was achieved. They witnessed the apogee, the decline, and the ruin of the dynasty.

CHAPTER X
THE SHRINE OF ROYAL MEMORIES, THE SCENE OF WORLD ADJUSTMENTS

It was not long after the enforced departure of Louis XVI and the Court that the immense sepulcher of regal glory was dismantled and forsaken. During the Revolution some of the furnishings were taken to Paris to supply the needs of the king and his family at the Tuileries. A number of pictures and objects of art contained in the palace and the two Trianons were removed to the Museum of the Louvre, which had been founded in 1775. Some of these paintings, including the _Joconde_ by da Vinci, and famous canvases by Titian, del Sarto, Rubens and Van Dyck, still hang on the walls of the first national gallery of France. Agitated discussions arose as to the final destiny of the palace and its contents. A group of law-makers would have sold the building outright. But in July, 1793, the Convention decreed the establishment at Versailles of a provincial school, a museum of art objects taken from the houses of those that had emigrated from troublous France, a public library, a French museum for painting and sculpture, and a natural history exhibition. There were, however, Revolutionaries that so despised the relics of royalty that they continued to urge from time to time the complete demolition of the palace and park-- chief works of Louis XIV's reign. The most diligent defenders of the chateau were the inhabitants of the town of Versailles, who were keenly aware that the continued existence of the palace would insure a measure of prosperity to the community. They protested, that, just object of the people's venom as the edifice was, it nevertheless stood as a monument to the arts and crafts of France during two centuries. The assailants that made hideous the days of October fifth and sixth, 1789, had done comparatively little material damage within the palace precincts. Gun shots of the Paris mob had disfigured two statues at the main entry to the courtyard, had destroyed the grill that separated the Royal Court from the Court of the Ministers; lunges of their bayonets had broken the mirrors in the Grand Gallery, while pursuing the Guards to massacre them. Otherwise, the historic walls and gardens bore no evidence of Revolutionary fury.

After several years of contention, plan and counter-plan, the Convention definitely saved Versailles for the nation by the decrees of 1794 and 1795. During this epoch of violence and revolt, thousands of articles were offered for sale at the stables of Versailles, in the presence of appointed representatives of the people. Linen, utensils, mirrors, clocks, cabinets, chandeliers, stoves, damask curtains, carriages, wines of Madeira, Malaga and Corinth, coffee, Sevres porcelains, engravings, paintings, drawings, and some fine furniture went for a song at this colossal auction. In 1796 the Minister of finance ordered that remaining pieces of furniture of great beauty and value be put on sale. In this way were summarily dispersed chairs of tapestry and gilt that would to-day command extravagant sums; desks of exquisite marquetry, at which kingly documents and _billets doux_ had been penned; dressing-tables whose mirrors had reflected the faces, sad or gay, frank or subtle, of queens and mistresses; wardrobes that had held the linens and brocades of princes and courtiers; clocks of gold and enamel that had registered the hours of portentous births and marriages. Tables of mosaic and satinwood, cushions of gold brocade, cameo medallions, porcelain panels, plaques of lacquer and bronze were included on the list of articles to be disposed of. In the original inventory, discovered in the library at Versailles, were included pieces of Saxony ware, Watteau figures, Sevres vases, dishes and cups, Beauvais tapestries, clocks made by Robin and de Sotian, candelabra of crystal, chandeliers of silver--all from the apartments of the King, the Queen and the Dauphin. For 20,000 francs there was sold a tapestry emblematic of the American Revolution. Creditors of the new Government were paid in furniture and art works whose value they estimated to please their own purses. A brochure published at Paris by Charles Davillier recites the romance of "The Sale of the Furnishings of Versailles during the Terror." To a certain Monsieur Lanchère, a former cab driver who had undertaken the conduct of military convoys and transports for the State, were assigned clocks, carpets, statuary, chests, secretaries and consoles that embarrassed every nook and corner of the spacious Paris mansion of which he became proprietor.

"Paris," narrates Monsieur Davillier, "was gorged after the sale at the chateau of Versailles with priceless furniture and objects of _vertu_." Newspapers were filled with the advertisements of second-hand dealers offering to the public these souvenirs--redolent, splendid, tragic--of a dead-and-gone dynasty, of an epoch vanished never to return.

The institutions whose establishment at Versailles definitely saved the chateau and its dependencies for posterity, were, at the Palace, a conservatory of arts and sciences and a library of 30,000 volumes; in the Kitchen Garden a school of gardening and husbandry; at the Grand Commune, a manufactory of arms; at the Menagerie, a school of agriculture. Halls that had echoed to the dance and the clink of gold at gaming-tables now heard profound lectures on history, ancient languages, mathematics, chemistry, and political economy! Classic exercises beneath the painted ceilings of these memoried rooms! Scholastic discourse where music and laughter had vibrated for a hundred extravagant years!

The galleries at the Louvre contributed to the new Versailles museum all the canvases of French artists that it possessed. Fragonard and Greuze, Lebrun, Claude Lorrain, Mignard, Poussin, Rigaud, Vanloo, Vernet--all were represented, some of them by numerous examples of their graceful art. Besides, there was a Rubens Gallery, and two salons filled with the works of Paul Veronese. Some of these treasures were later removed to the Luxembourg Palace, where the French Senate was sitting, and to the palace of Saint-Cloud, residence of Napoleon Bonaparte, First Consul. Little by little the canvases were dispersed, until, at the end of the Empire, the Versailles Museum of French Art ceased to be.

At the beginning of the year 1800, Napoleon Bonaparte established at Versailles a branch of the _Hôtel des Invalides_ in Paris, and wounded veterans of the Revolution to the number of 2,000 were installed for two years in the vast apartments of Louis XV and in rooms overlooking the garden and the Court of Ministers. During this period several of the salons were opened to the people for exhibitions and assemblies, and the public were free to enjoy the park, the Orangery and the fragrant bosques of Trianon. Fêtes of the Republic frequently took place about a national altar raised near the Lake of the Swiss Guards, and a Tree of Liberty was planted with great solemnity in the court of the château, where the equestrian statue of Louis XIV now stands. In illuminating contrast to the regal celebrations it succeeded was this latter ceremony, which was inaugurated by a meeting in the historic Tennis Court, where loyal republicans took a new oath of hatred for all things royal, and swore devotion to the constitution. Into the dwelling of former sovereigns the people then crowded to witness the ceremony of breaking a scepter and crown into a thousand pieces. Next, they gathered around the Liberty Oak to consecrate it; they hung it with ribbons of the tricolor of France, a band played "a republican air," and an orator delivered a speech in commemoration of the glorious anniversary of the day on which "the last tyrant of the French" had been guillotined. Fortunately for the peace of mind of the Sixteenth Louis, he had no gift of prevision!

With the beginning of Napoleon's reign, Versailles and the Trianon became once more part of the Crown lands. The Emperor ordered necessary repairs to be made. In the theater the royal troupe of comedians was sometimes heard. The canal, which had nearly dried up during the neglectful rule of the Republic, was again filled with water. The park and the facades of the palace were restored, and in the Gallery and State Apartments artists renewed the colors of the mural decorations. Many of the repairs and changes made by Dufour, Napoleon's architect, have remained to the present time. Certain parts of the palace giving on the courts were in ruins, Louis XV and his heir having had no money to spare for their restoration. In 1811, after the Peace of Vienna, Napoleon, then in residence at the Grand Trianon, took under advisement the complete reconstruction of the palace. In consternation he surveyed the tumbling walls and the general confusion that confronted him during one of his promenades in the park and Orangery. "Why," cried he, "did the Revolution, which destroyed everything else, spare the chateau of Versailles! Then I would not have had on my hands this embarrassing legacy from Louis XIV--an old chateau poorly built--one much favored without just cause."

Architects busied themselves with innumerable plans for re-making the shabby pile. Some would have torn down the Council Hall, the bedchamber of Louis XIV, the antechamber of the Bull's Eye, and all the rest of the palace except the apartments of the King and Queen, the Gallery with the salons at either end, the Chapel and the Opera House. Napoleon was willing to spend 6,000 francs on the construction of suites for himself and his family "and fifty others." "Then," said he, "we could perhaps come to Versailles to pass a summer." The disasters of the year 1812 and the fall of the Empire saved the palace from the threatened renovation.

When Louis XVIII ascended the throne of his Bourbon ancestors after the extinction of Napoleon's Star of Hope, he conceived a new plan "to put the chateau of Versailles in a habitable state." During the next six years (1814-1820) the King restored the Hall of Mirrors and all that was especially associated with Louis XIV. He finished the facade on the Paris side, begun by Gabriel under Louis XV, and built a pavilion corresponding to the one designed and erected by this same architect. He did away with a maze of small apartments, cleaned and simplified the interior, restored painted ceilings and gilt embellishments, and with great care put in order the entire palace and its surroundings. The chapel was repaired and blessed anew by the Bishop of Strassbourg.

Many State visitors came to see Versailles, even in the days when it was shorn of its glory. Pope Pius VII was there in 1805. From the balcony outside the Gallery of Mirrors he bestowed his benediction upon a crowd that stood below on the terraces. Two days later the Salon of Hercules was the scene of a ball in celebration of the coronation of the first Emperor of France. In May, 1814, Czar Alexander I of Russia visited Versailles with his two brothers, following the example of Peter the Great, who had been there when Louis XV was on the throne. Another historic cortège was composed of Frederick William III of Prussia and his two sons, one of whom, Prince William, was to return to Versailles in the year 1870 on a mission less peaceful. The gates of Versailles opened to the Duke of Wellington in 1818.

Other visitors there were that came to Versailles and, by the good will of Louis XVIII, lodged there--homeless dependents, who dried their laundry at the stately windows of the palace and installed goats and cows on the roofs overlooking the inert bronze fountains.

After the reign of Charles X all the occupants at the chateau left, following the Revolution of July, 1830. Once more the question arose as to the disposition of the palace. Empty, abandoned, "What shall we do with it?" cried the ministers. The answer was found in the project proposed to Louis Philippe that Versailles should become a national depository for souvenirs of French history, surrounded by the splendors of Louis the Great. This suggestion had the king's approval and cooperation. A confusion of offices, rooms, staircases and passages was simplified in the two wings, and the main body of the chateau and long galleries were created for the reception of thousands of battle pictures, portraits and pieces of sculpture, reflecting events and personalities concerned with the story of France.

The Queen's bed-chamber, the apartments of Madame de Maintenon and of the daughters of Louis XV and Madame de Pompadour were among those that were altered. In the entrance court of the chateau were placed a group of statues from the Paris bridge _de la Concorde_, all of them so massive that they were out of proportion to the low surrounding walls.

On the face of the north and south wings Louis Philippe caused to be engraved the dedication of the huge pile and its contents "To all the Glories of France." The sum expended under the direction of the architect, Nepveu, for the creation of the National Museum of Versailles, exceeded 20,000,000 francs (about $4,000,000). The inauguration of the museum in June, 1837, was attended by Louis Philippe and his Queen, by officers of the Army and Government and representatives of French Law, Commerce, Art and Education. Arriving from Trianon, where they had been in residence, the King and his wife entered the palace by the Marble Stairway, traversed the Grand Hall of the Guards (to-day called the Hall of Napoleon) and the halls leading to the Grand Gallery of Battles, where they saw portrayed on canvas all the important military engagements of French armies, from Tolbiac to Wagram. In the Chamber of Louis XIV the King and Queen examined the restorations of the furniture, and found them well done. A royal banquet was laid in the Grand Gallery and in adjacent salons. At eight o'clock His Majesty, the royal family and 1500 guests assembled in the brilliantly illuminated Opera House, where they witnessed a performance of Molière's _Misanthrope_ and extracts from the opera, _Robert le Diable_, by Meyerbeer. The spectacle was concluded by a piece written by Eugene Scribe, the famous French librettist, in celebration of the founding of the Museum. At midnight the King and his family led a procession through the galleries of the palace, lighted by footmen carrying torches. At two o'clock in the morning the festivities were at an end and the royal party left for Trianon.

Says a French author, writing two years after the opening of the museum. "When Louis Philippe first cast his eye upon Versailles, he saw at once the impiety of allowing such a monument to sink into utter ruin.... He determined that the palace of Louis XIV, without losing its individuality, should become a palace of the entire people; and that the bygone spirit of absolutism should give shelter to the spirit of modern liberty. Versailles, therefore, erected as a homage to individual pride, has become, under the Orleans regime, a great national monument--and certainly the most complete and splendid of its class in all Europe. The temple of luxury was converted into a temple of the arts, and French valor was recorded in immortal colors upon the walls, by French genius."

In the vast edifice Louis Philippe created a pictorial record that embraced not only the great battles from the beginning of the monarchy down to his own day, but the chief incidents that distinguished the reigns of Louis XIV, XV and XVI; the victories of the Republic; the campaigns of Napoleon; the reigns of Louis XVIII and Charles X; the Revolution of 1830, and the reign of Louis Philippe. The kings of France, the members of their families and immediate entourage, great French warriors, statesmen, artists, men of letters and science are depicted on canvases that line the immense halls of Versailles. The Gallery of Warriors was arranged by Louis Philippe in that part of the palace formerly occupied by Madame de Montespan. The Gallery of Napoleon, created by removing the partition from a dozen rooms belonging to various members of the royal family, presents a complete history of the Emperor's life. More than a hundred apartments, large and small, were obliterated to make room for the galleries of portraits--a most engrossing exhibition to students of French history. Carlyle said, "I have found that the Portrait was a small lighted candle by which the Biographies could for the first time be read, and some human interpretation be made of them."

Unfortunately a considerable number of paintings hung in the new museum suffered in quality through the desire of Louis Philippe to bring his achievement to immediate completion. He gave commissions right and left, always with the stipulation that the artists _make haste_. But many canvases of high merit, artistically and historically, still grace the walls of these galleries.

Portraits of the four unmarried daughters of Louis XV have been appropriately arranged by the present curator of Versailles, Monsieur de Nolhac, in the apartments on the ground floor where Mesdames passed most of their dull, insignificant lives. Nattier made flattering representations of all of them, sometimes in the costume of mythological characters. Both Nattier and the great La Tour portrayed Marie Leczinska, the mother of Louis XV's ten children. Nattier's likeness shows a smiling, matronly lady with sweet-tempered brown eyes, seated in a chair, the face softened by a frill and a black lace scarf. Many of the portraits at Versailles painted by Charles Lebrun, Madame Vigée Lebrun, Jean-Baptiste and Michel Vanloo, Boucher, Largillière, Pierre Mignard, Rigaud, are familiar to us through frequent reproduction.

In the years following the inauguration of the National Museum, Versailles was once again the scene of ostentatious fêtes in the halls, gardens and splendid Opera House. When Louis Napoleon succeeded Louis Philippe as head of the French nation, he came to Versailles with his bride of three days, the beautiful Eugénie, to see the portraits of Marie Antoinette, for whom the young Empress cherished a special admiration.

On an August night in 1855, "the grand court of the château shone with a brilliance resembling day. The profile of the great edifice was outlined in small lights. In the gardens, arches and columns were raised and the fountains showered rainbow torrents. The Hall of Mirrors presented a spectacle whose splendor recalled nights when Louis XIV strolled here in brocade and ruffles. Garlands hung from the ceiling, thousands of lights reproduced themselves in the lofty mirrors and shed scintillating floods upon the handsome costumes of the invited ones." Thus the _Moniteur Universel_ described to its readers the reception offered by the Emperor of France to Queen Victoria, the Prince Consort and the future King of England. A few years later Emperor Napoleon III commanded another fête amid the grandeurs of Versailles, this time in honor of the King of Spain.

But the days and nights of royal spectacles at last came to an end--and for all time. In the month of September, 1870, the chateau offered refuge to German soldiers wounded in the short but bitter war with France. In the _Oeil-de-Boeuf_, the Council Hall, the little apartments of Louis XV and those of Marie Antoinete were placed four hundred invalid cots. By October, Bismarck arrived in the town of Versailles. During the next five months he resided on the Rue de Provence, in the villa of Madame Jessé, widow of a prosperous cloth manufacturer. His quarters were the center of diplomatic action during the period that preceded the signing of the shameful peace terms. January 18, 1871, the anniversary of the day on which the first king of Prussia had crowned himself at Konigsberg (1701), was fixed for the proclamation of William II as German Emperor, in the Hall of Mirrors. In the phrase of a chronicler of that time, "It was impossible for the boldest imagination to picture a more thorough revenge on the traditional foes of Germany than the proclamation of the German Empire in the storied palace of the Kings of France. With the shades of

Richelieu and the Grand Monarch looking down upon them did the Teutonic chieftains raise as it were, their leader on their shields, and with clash of arms and martial music acclaim him kaiser of a re-united Germany." King William passed from the altar in the middle of the Gallery to a platform at the end of the hall and there took his place before the colors, surrounded "by a brilliant multitude of princes, generals, officers and troops." When he had announced the re-establishment of the Empire, and when Bismarck, "looking pale, but calm and self-possessed," had read to the assemblage the Proclamation to the German people, "the bands burst forth with the national anthem, colors and helmets were wildly waved, and the Hall of Mirrors shook with a tremendous shout that was taken up and swelled till the rippling thunder-roll of cheers struck the ears of the startled watchers on the walls of Paris," where roar of cannon night and day summoned the French to surrender. Thus the German Empire was born at the very seat of French Monarchy.

The armistice terms were signed at Versailles on the twenty-eighth day of January. One month later the representative of stricken France and Bismarck, sitting in the Chancellor's headquarters, affixed their signatures to the Peace Preliminaries, by which France surrendered Alsace (except Belfort) and Lorraine, and agreed to pay within three years a war indemnity of five thousand million francs.[*]

After the departure of the Prussians from Versailles (March 12, 1871), the Deputies of France arrived from Bordeaux, the temporary capital, and lodged in the Hall of Mirrors, which then became a dormitory, as it had on occasion been a hospital ward, a ball-room and the banqueting hall of royalty.

The insurrection of the Commune of Paris compelled the ministers to seek a place of security at Versailles. Once more the palace was chosen as the seat of Government. The ground floor, the upper floor and the attic, the picture galleries, even the vestibule of the Queen's Stairway and the servants' quarters served as offices for ministers and secretaries. The Department of Justice was installed in the Guards' Hall, the _Oeil-de-Boeuf_ and the rooms of Marie Antoinette. The Secretary of Public Works directed his affairs within walls that had sheltered the nefarious Dubarry. The official _Journal_ was printed in the palace kitchens. For several years the Opera House, the north wing, and the intimate apartments of Louis XV were given over to the National Assembly.

A Republican fête offered in 1878 by the president, Marshal MacMahon, was attended by twelve thousand guests. Once more the fountains of the north parterre were illuminated, but this time with electric bulbs instead of oil lanterns. There were ingenious fireworks on the _Tapis-Vert_ that would have astounded even the courtiers of the Grand Monarch. In the _Galerie des Glaces_, Dussieux tells us, there was a ball "not exclusively aristocratic, but nevertheless very gay and animated."

Within the past forty years the treasury of the French Republic has not infrequently been taxed for repairs at Versailles and Trianon. More than a million francs were spent on the chapel alone. Improvements in the park, including the restoration of the Basin of Neptune, the Orangery and the Colonnade, cost another million.

"This Versailles," exclaims a French author, "does it not attract to our country strangers without number, does it not lend lasting prestige to the land of France? . . . Outside of the Invalides and the Louvre, what edifices equal it in evoking the memorable periods with which they are associated? What lasting respect do these annals of stone and bronze merit from men of taste! These salons, gardens, statues, works of art, attached irrevocably to the Past, bid us pause and ponder long upon the matchless Story of Versailles."

[*]The final treaty of peace between France and Germany was signed in the Swan Hotel at Frankfort, Germany, on May 10, 1871.

Milton Keynes UK
Ingram Content Group UK Ltd.
UKHW042107131124
451149UK00006B/694